Beside Still Waters...

A Growing Gold Book

Beside Still Waters...

❖

Shepherding in the New Millennium

Dr. Charles E. Smith

Writer's Showcase
San Jose New York Lincoln Shanghai

Beside Still Waters...
Shepherding in the New Millennium

Writer's Showcase
an imprint of iUniverse, Inc.

For information address:
iUniverse, Inc.
5220 S. 16th St., Suite 200
Lincoln, NE 68512
www.iuniverse.com

Scriptural References

Unless otherwise indicated, all Scriptural passages are taken from the New International Version.

ISBN: 0-595-23638-3

Printed in the United States of America

This book is dedicated to all who shepherd human sheep, who give themselves in a potent and selfless manner that sheep in their care may know abundant life.

Contents

Acknowledgements

Many people contribute to the writing of a book. While the author usually comes up with the pivotal idea around which to weave a story, nonetheless, he or she draws upon the life, experience, and abilities of others to produce a finished product.

I have been blessed with the support and encouragement of the one who shares my life, and the friendship of many, in particular, that of Jim Vernon over whose table many of the ideas found in this book were discussed and Julie Wolpers who always found time to diagnose and cure the ills of a recalcitrant computer.

Introduction

The Shepherd's Psalm is perhaps Scripture's most loved passage. Timeless in relevance and application, it affirms the Lord is our Shepherd as He was the shepherd of the Psalmist, that we are sheep of His flock.

In both Old and New Testaments, shepherd is the metaphor most often used to depict God's relationship to Man. David, Isaiah, Jeremiah, and Ezekiel all portray Jehovah as a shepherd who leads, watches over, and rescues his sheep, gathering the lambs in His arms, and gently leading those who are with young.

Because the figures of shepherd and sheep are so strong and their relationship such an intimate one, it is possible that in the Shepherd's Psalm is prefigured the work of the Good Shepherd and the life He came to bring members of the human flock. It is for reasons like these, perhaps, that Jesus chose the metaphor of the shepherd to establish Himself as Messiah in the minds of the people.

As the world embarks upon its journey across the Twenty-First Century, the need is great for men and women to respond to the voice calling them to the vocation of shepherd.

This is especially true of nations like the United States where for better than a half century forces of transition and change have been reweaving the fabric of society, restructuring its institutions, and stretching people and their relationships to the limit.

Fueled by technology, change has avalanched upon us making us more efficient and productive in our work, altering our view of time, redefining play, revolutionizing the way we communicate, and contributing to the growth of relational vacuums in society making it more difficult to connect in friendship with others.

Carried along by currents of transition and change, Americans have let go, lost, or left behind important beliefs, traditions, practices, and principles called roots, among them religion as cultural cement.

Consequently, America's connection with the life of the spirit is tenuous. In the wake of extraordinary shifts in spiritual consciousness and social orientation, America lacks a solid foundation upon which to base its national life. As a consequence, society and its people seek meaning, purpose, happiness, peace, and a sense of personal worth and value in things external to themselves rather than within.

◆　　　◆　　　◆

There are challenges to shepherding human sheep in times of transition and change. Looming large among these is the reality that many members of the human flock are not enjoying the life Jesus came to bring them, some because they are hungry, others because they are fearful, many because of tension in their relationships, and numerous others because they have wandered from the paths of righteousness and are cast down in their souls.

Chapter One is an investigation of the relationship of shepherd and sheep.

Chapter Two explores what shepherds must do to be effective shepherds of human sheep in an ambitious, aggressive, technologically driven society.

With Chapter Three the focus shifts to the Beatitudes of Matthew and Luke in which are found traits and characteristics of the ideal disciple and citizen of the Kingdom of God and the blessings promised those who manifest the spiritual, moral, qualities and attributes they contain.

Each Beatitudinal chapter ends with "Notes for Shepherds," a special section containing suggestions for becoming the kind of person whom God seeks to bless.

1

The Lord Is My Shepherd

With the possible exception of Paul's incomparable description of love in the Thirteenth Chapter of First Corinthians, and Koheleth's perspective on time and life in Ecclesiastes Chapter Three, the Shepherd's Psalm is perhaps the most familiar, most loved, and most quoted passage in all of Scripture.

It opens with the sheep declaring, *"The Lord is my shepherd, I shall not want."*

Under most circumstances, a declaration of this kind spoken by a sheep would be pure hyperbole. However, with a minimum understanding of sheep and an awareness of the intimate, affectionate, personal nature of the relationship shepherds have with sheep, *"I shall not want"* is a statement of reality.

Old and New Testaments Writers Used the Metaphor of Shepherd for God

The metaphor of the shepherd is scattered throughout both Old and New Testaments. In Psalm Twenty-Three, David identifies Jehovah as shepherd. The prophet Isaiah speaks of Jehovah as a shepherd who leads his flock and gathers the lambs in his arms, carrying them close to heart, gently leading those that are with young (Isaiah 40:11).

Jeremiah depicts Jehovah as a shepherd who watches over His flock (Jeremiah 31:10), while Ezekiel portrays Jehovah as a shepherd who looks after and rescues his flock (Ezekiel 34:12). Highly significant is the fact that when Jehovah's relationship with humankind is the focus

3

of the writers of Scripture, the metaphor used more than any other is
the metaphor of the shepherd.

Jesus identified Himself as the "Good Shepherd" who came to bring
abundant life to human sheep. He used the metaphor of shepherd to
establish Himself as Messiah in the minds of the people, and wove into
His teachings the several views of shepherds found in the Old Testament.

The confidence of the sheep reflects the commitment shepherds
have to sheep in their care. Knowing the shepherd is committed to
meeting their needs, sheep declare, *"I shall not want"* because:

- He makes me lie down in green pastures

- He leads me beside still waters

- He restores my soul

- He leads me in the paths of righteousness.

Each statement merits individual attention and comment.

'He Makes Me Lie Down in Green Pastures'

The land of the Bible, the region known as Palestine covers an area of
approximately 12,000 square miles, stretching one hundred fifty miles
North to South (Dan to Beersheba generally accepted as traditional
boundaries of Israel) and eighty miles East to West.[1]

The Holy Land is a semiarid region in which pastures for grazing
sheep are scarce. Locating pastures for sheep is a never-ending task and
when suitable ones are not to be had, they must be cultivated.

Pastures for grazing sheep are critically important as sheep will not
lie down as long as they are hungry, will forage until their stomachs are
full, graze the same areas repeatedly, and skim the grass to ground level.

A good deal of the friction between cattlemen and sheepmen in the
American southwest during the late Nineteenth Century is directly
related to the inclination of sheep to crop the grass down to ground

level. Already at odds with farmers whom they ridiculed as "sod busters" because farmers carved up the range with their plows, cattlemen loathed sheep and were contemptuous of those who raised them. In the minds of men whose livelihood depended upon cattle, sheep destroyed the range.

Even when pastures are plentiful sheep will not lie down as long as they are afraid. Sheep are fearful, apprehensive creatures. They cannot relax if there is the slightest hint of danger as they have little or no way of defending themselves. In the face of danger, the only option available to sheep is to run, and they can't do that very well.

◆   ◆   ◆

During the summer months, shepherds move their flocks from one area to another in search of fresh pastures. This journey can be as hazardous for shepherds as it is for sheep as many times the way is through stretches of jagged, broken, uneven terrain in which wind and rain have chiseled crevasses and ravines that provide ideal cover for predators and robbers. The Psalmist refers to such places as *The Valley of the Shadow of Death*, or more accurately, *The Valley of Dark Shadows*.

However demanding and dangerous the journey, however, sheep are unafraid because of the comforting and reassuring presence of the shepherd. *"I will fear no evil,"* declares the sheep, *"for thou art with me."*

And when the flock emerges unscathed and unharmed from the Valley of Dark Shadows, sheep are free to enjoy the table prepared for them by the shepherd in the presence of their enemies.

To understand the meaning of the phrase, *"You prepare a table before me in the presence of mine enemies,"* the scene is best visualized from above.

From this perspective what one sees is a fairly level grassy plane resembling the surface of a table from which sheep are free to eat in the presence of their enemies who remain on the slopes leading to The Valley of Dark Shadows through which the flock has just passed.

◆   ◆   ◆

As flocks move from one pasture to another, shepherds allocate a great deal of time and energy to the task of forging a bond with sheep in their care. One way they have of doing this is by spending a part of the day with each member of the flock.

At some point during the day, shepherds single out a particular member of the flock. Placing the leather tip of their staff alongside its head, shepherd and sheep stroll along in the same way humans walk when holding hands, the shepherd talking, or, perhaps, singing to the sheep as cowboys talked and sang to cattle on drives across prairies of the American Southwest.

◆   ◆   ◆

Daily contacts like the one described serve purposes beyond that of forging a relational bond. They also condition sheep to recognize the voice of the shepherd.

Each human voice has a distinctive tonal quality called "timbre." Sheep respond to the call of their shepherd because they recognize the tonal quality of his voice. They will not respond to shepherds other than their own because the tonal quality of their voices is different from that of their shepherd.

The ability of sheep to identify their voice is extremely useful to the shepherd. When predators threaten, sudden changes in weather necessitate gathering sheep together quickly, or, as occasionally happens, flocks are housed together for the night, all that is required to separate one flock from another is for each shepherd to call to his sheep.

◆   ◆   ◆

In contrast to sheep, humans appear unaware of presence as an essential attribute of their humanness, therefore, unable to appreciate the fact that inherent in their presence is power to connect with the spirit of others.

This lack of awareness and/or appreciation of presence as a facet of humanness can be attributed, in part, to extraordinary shifts in spiritual consciousness and social orientation brought about by social forces unleashed in the years following World War II.

Alvin Toffler warned of things to come in his thought provoking book, *Future Shock*. *"Change,"* he said, *"is avalanching upon our heads and most people are grotesquely unprepared to cope with it."* [2]

Future shock is what happens when society and its people are subjected to "too much change in too short a time," when the future invades the present at such velocity and with such force that scarcely is one wave of change incorporated into the lives of people before another crashes in upon them.[3]

For over half a century Americans have been living the reality Toffler anticipated. Like waves rolling upon the shore, social forces set in motion by World War II progressively gathered momentum, in time becoming the "roaring current of change" that continues to this day to reweave the fabric of society, restructure its institutions, and stretch the flexibility of society and its people to their limits.

It would have been impossible to anticipate the changes that would avalanche upon Americans before the dawning of the Twenty-First Century. Certainly, emerging from a Second World War we were ill-prepared for such things as:

- Artificial hearts, organ transplants, and the "pill"
- Nuclear energy and laser beams
- Credit cards and ATMs
- Ballpoint pens, disposable razors and cameras
- Frozen food, air conditioners, and permanent press clothes
- Clothes dryers, electric blankets, and panty hose

- Computers, modems, cellular phones, and the Internet
- Turn signals, fuel injection, anti-lock brakes, and heated windshields
- Weather and information satellites, and
- Moon landings.

Even before the publication of *Future Shock*, a change of historical significance had taken place sometime in the mid-1950s, when the United States became the first major power in the world in which *"more than 50 percent of the non-farm labor force ceased to wear the blue collar of factory or manual labor."*[4]

This shift is significant, for however unprepared Americans may have been for change, social forces were transforming the nation from an industrial to the post-modern, super-technological society in which we live.

◆   ◆   ◆

William Bridges is a pioneer in the study of human transitions. He became interested in this area when forced to address bewildering changes in his own life.

At age forty-one, Bridges was losing interest in his career of undergraduate teaching. Relationship with his wife was not good. In fact, there were times when it was questionable whether their marriage would last.

Depressed and frightened, needing to make sense of the unexpected and disorienting changes taking place, Bridges left his position as Professor of English at Mills College, went into intensive psychotherapy, and formed an intentional community with five other families.

In time, Bridges' experience evolved into a series of seminars, and, belatedly, into a book appropriately titled, *Transitions*, in which he defined transition as *"the natural process of disorientation and reorientation that marks the turning points of the path of growth,"* and *"transitions"* as *"unavoidable slices of life experience which our culture does little to help us prepare for or understand."*[5]

Whether viewed as unavoidable slices of life experience, turning points in the path of growth, or opportunities for self renewal, transitions can be arduous, painful, and threatening because change becomes a way of life.

For a variety of reasons we resist change as often as we embrace it. Sometimes we resist for sentimental reasons. Who among us, for instance, has not returned to the home of their childhood only to discover the tree in the backyard is not as large as we remembered it? Or, who among us has not attended a High School class reunion knowing time changes everyone, yet wanting to see our classmates as we remembered them?

We resist change for reasons other than the ones mentioned above. We resist because

- Change involves loss of some kind

- It threatens our security, and

- We are programmed to equate the familiar with good and perceive that which is new as threatening.

Many people could foresee technology enabling the work force of the country to be more efficient and productive, thus creating the possibility of a shorter workweek and more leisure time.

Yet, for all its promise, technology has neither shortened our workweek nor given us more leisure time. A recent article in *Psychology Today* confirms that, in fact, we work more hours today than ten years ago, technology having added nine additional hours to our workweek. Little wonder forty percent of participants in a recent study reported themselves rushed for time, breathless from coping with frantic schedules.[6]

◆   ◆   ◆

While many individuals anticipated the influence of technology on the productivity and efficiency of the workplace, few envisioned technology altering our view of time, revamping the way we communicate with each other, and creating relational vacuums within society.

◆   ◆   ◆

Technology has redefined time. No longer is time *"the longest distance between two places,"* as it was for Tennessee Williams, or a crucible *"...in which all things pass away,"* as it was for Schopenhauer, or *"...a fluid condition which has no existence except in the momentary avatars of individual people,"* as William Faulkner thought of it.[7] Time has become a resource used to produce results that can be measured.

◆   ◆   ◆

Technology has also redefined play, changed its purpose, and altered our approach to it. *"Play,"* says Professor Godbey of Penn State University, *"is fooling around,"* losing ourselves in an activity, oblivious and unconcerned over the possibility that we might make a fool of ourselves.[8]

In times past, play was purposeless fooling around. The intent of play was to enjoy oneself. People played with abandon because play was not expected to produce anything. Today, play has become *"a thing, a commodity, an event undertaken at a specific time for a specific purpose."*[9] We no longer play with abandon as we have a hard time *"allowing ourselves the purposelessness that is absolutely fundamental"* to play.[10]

When play ceases to be purposeless fooling around, it becomes work. When abandon is lost the reward of play is no longer play itself, but something that can be measured.

◆   ◆   ◆

While a number of people anticipated technology increasing efficiency and productivity in the market place, and a limited number visualized technology changing our view of time and play, few anticipated technology revolutionizing communication so completely that the present age would bear the label, "The Age of Communication."

We communicate with such speed and ease that war has become a spectator activity and with such frequency that the subtitle assigned the present time is "The Age of Interruption."

◆   ◆   ◆

Of all the ways technology has impacted society, however, none was less anticipated than the way technology would emphasize being able to read. While in times past one could get by without knowing how to read, technology not only demands that we read, but that we read more than ever before.

A case in point is the personal computer. Every computer comes with one or more manuals the buyer must read if he or she is to derive maximum benefit from capabilities built into it.

◆   ◆   ◆

Bridges' research suggests the experience of individuals, society, and nations in transition are similar in that transitions take place in phases. They begin with an ending, continue through a period of uncertainty, and are completed in new beginnings.

Transitions Begin With An Ending

During the initial phase of transition, individuals, society, and nations let go of things familiar to them, things that give them identity and a feeling of belonging. They let go of routines and lifestyles associated with the place they are living. They cease pursuing some goals and objectives. They close some gestalts because its time to bring other things to the forefront.

A recent television commercial promoting the services of a nationwide van line illustrates this point effectively. In the commercial a husband and wife are walking through a house emptied of furnishings. They pause to examine marks on the facing of a door chronicling the growth of their children. The wife wipes a tear from her eye and the couple embrace before walking out the door. The van drives away.

Transition for the couple in the commercial probably involved letting go of a circle of friends: couples, singles, golfing buddies, bridge partners, service clubs, baby sitters, the grocer, mailman, a few store owners, and most likely, a place of worship familiar to them.

Transitions Involve Uncertainty

The middle period of transitions is characterized by confusion and distress, lostness and emptiness. As people disconnect from aspects of their past, it is as if they are putting out to sea with no compass. Uncertain as to the meaning and purpose of their experience, the future they face is about as clear to them as a distant object viewed through a camera whose viewfinder is out of focus.

Transitions Lead To New Beginnings

The experience of individuals, society, and nations in transition is also alike in that the uncertainty of the middle period is usually followed by a phase of reorientation and new beginnings.

New beginnings are attempts at reorienting oneself in a new reality, restoring order and direction, purpose and pace to life.

Arriving at their destination, the family in the commercial will establish new routines, once again becoming participants in activities designed to give them identity and bring them a sense of belonging. They will seek out a new place of worship, associate with new service and community organizations, and build new relationships.

◆   ◆   ◆

Bridges' findings are consistent with America in transition. Making the transition from an industrial to a super-technological society Americans have let go, lost, or left behind a number of important beliefs, traditions, practices, and principles called "roots."

Roots serve as guidelines for our lives. They bind society and its people together and because they are generally shared by a majority of people, bring continuity and consistency to life.

Less recognized, but no less important, roots help us decide what we want to say with our lives. One of the more devastating results of having disconnected from our roots is that while our young people know what they want to do with their lives, they don't know what they want to say with them.

◆   ◆   ◆

Religion as cultural cement is one of the roots left behind in the transition to a post-modern society. In times past, belief in God governed the way people organized their lives and their cities. Life was organized around rituals that affirmed belief in God (prayer, meditation, confession, penance, and pilgrimage), while cities were organized around institutions through which people demonstrated their belief. Included among these: the Church, monastery, school, and hospice.

In making the transition to a super-technological society, belief in God (in which the emphasis is on the inner life of spirit) has weakened considerably. As early as the 1970s, when asked by *Newsweek* magazine to respond to the question, "What ails the American Spirit?" several prominent historians and professors of government referred to the diminished role of religion.

A decade after the query by *Newsweek*, historian Richard Nisbett spoke of religion as a spent force in America. It was his opinion that *"We have,"* in the words of Jonathan Swift, *"just enough religion to make us hate but not enough to make us love one another…enough to make us see the flaws and cankers of the society around us but not enough to generate hope for the future."*[11]

◆   ◆   ◆

As America moves into the Twenty-First Century it is a nation whose connection with the life of the spirit is tenuous. Religion no longer functions as cultural cement for society and its people, nor does it bring meaning and continuity to human experience in the same way and to the same extent it once did.

Lacking the cement that once helped us determine what we want to say with our lives, Americans pursue meaning, purpose, direction, and a sense of personal worth and value in things external to themselves.

Yet, because such things are not found in anything external to ourselves, thousands travel the road of addiction and acquisition in a society in which addictive behavior is said to be the norm.[12]

◆   ◆   ◆

In all likelihood, technology will continue to fuel the pace and influence the direction of society and its people. To live abundantly Americans need to identify aspects of technology that are beneficial and helpful and aspects likely to stretch them beyond the limits of their flexibility.

To live abundantly Americans need a vision of themselves as spiritual beings and a commitment to a way of life that places value on the inner life of the spirit.

Spirit is the essence of life breathed into humankind at Creation. It is the presence of God in human life, the "life" of life itself, formless and incorporeal, boundless and limitless.

Spirit is formless because it is energy, incorporeal because it has no substance to be seen, touched, and weighed, boundless and limitless because it can live independent of the body.

Spirit is also that aspect of our being that makes it possible to know God, to commune with Him, and lay hold of things eternal. It is also the realm in which genuine worship takes place.

With this understanding, John 4:24 might readily be expanded to read:

"The God who has created us is spirit. He cannot be seen [for Spirit has no form] or touched [for Spirit has no substance that can be detected] unless He chooses to materialize Himself as Christ did in the upper room following His resurrection. Those who worship this God, must worship Him in spirit [their spirit must connect with His spirit] and in truth [the truth of who He is], for the Father seeks such [people who worship in the spirit] to worship Him."

Spirit manifests itself as "presence" in the lives of people. We are drawn to people who exhibit it because they radiate a power that transforms any setting in which they happen to be. Of such persons we say, "They have a good spirit," because their presence energizes, empowers, and invigorates.

It is easy to connect with individuals whose presence speaks loudly. In their company tension is reduced and anxiety lessened; barriers to communication and self-disclosure are lowered, and masks worn to hide aspects of ourselves that we would rather others not see, are removed.

Presence is what children need when uncertain or fearful. It is what Jimmy P. was needing the evening he disobeyed his parents repeatedly by getting out of bed and wandering into the living room where, late at night, his Father and Mother talked over events of the day.

After telling him to go back to bed several times, Jimmy's exasperated Mother took him by the hand and led him to his bedroom where, hands on hips, she announced, "Jimmy, I'm going to spank you if you get out of bed again. Your nightlight is on and you've got Pooh bear. So, go to sleep."

Her reprimand delivered, Jimmy's Mother turned to leave the room. As she turned off the light, Jimmy said, "Mom, Pooh bear's fine, but I want something with skin on it."

Presence is the cornerstone of human relationships. The presence of the shepherd comforts the sheep because of their relationship. Similarly, the presence of parents comforts and reassures children like Jimmy when they are fearful because of their relationship.

Presence comforts and reassures individuals who have experienced loss and/or passing through times of personal crisis and testing by validating them as persons of worth and value in spite of what the circumstances, situations, and conditions of their lives might suggest.

Presence is particularly comforting and reassuring to individuals struggling in the area of faith. A crisis of faith can be a lonely and potentially devastating experience even within the Body of Christ as there are some who view sin as the primary (if not the only) reason people struggle in their faith. Overlooked is the fact that people also struggle because they are growing in their faith.

◆   ◆   ◆

All in all, technology is something of a paradox in that at the same time it is providing tools that enable us to be more efficient and productive it is diminishing opportunities for connecting with others in friendship, thus contributing to the creation of relational vacuums that quickly become breeding grounds of loneliness.

Evidence of these vacuums is plentiful. Whereas, in a manufacturing society business was conducted face-to-face and transactions sealed with a handshake, a major portion of today's commerce is conducted by computer, conference call, or fax. Parties to business transactions know each other's voice and recognize each other's signature, yet rarely set eyes upon each other. In addition, countless thousands of individuals spend their working hours staring at the screen of a computer monitor and have no people contact at all.

Whereas, in an industrial society, families took at least one meal together (most likely the evening meal), in a super-technological society families rarely enjoy a meal together. As the pace of life quickens and the scope of activities enlarges for everyone, increasingly home is a place where family members have their transfers punched on their way to the next activity.

These observations point to a matter of increasing concern, namely, the rapid growth of relational aloneness as a condition within society.

The Old Testament teaches us, *"It is not good to be alone."* (Genesis 2:18) We are relationally alone anytime we feel (or actually are) cut off from, out of fellowship and communication with, unrelated to, or perhaps, unloved by persons from whom, under ordinary circumstances, we might reasonably expect to connect in order to have our needs met.

Humans fear aloneness. It is difficult enough to be physically alone, but when one is also relationally alone, life is especially tough.

No where is relational aloneness as apparent as it is on television talk shows where routinely more than one person talks simultaneously, and sometimes heatedly, each person attempting to prevail over the other by the sheer volume, velocity, and directness of their words, neither person paying much heed to what the other is saying nor particularly concerned that the words they speak might be hurting ones.

Relational aloneness is what Janice G. had been experiencing when she turned to her husband in the counselor's office one day and with considerable determination said, *"John, I need your p-r-e-s-e-n-c-e, not your p-r-e-s-e-n-t-s."* Obviously confounded and puzzled by his wife's words, John said, *"I don't understand, I work hard to give you everything you want."*

Feeling it important to intervene, the counselor said, *"John, your wife acknowledges you provide well for her and she appreciates that. What she is saying is, 'I don't need a new car, a new dining room suite, a new anything.' I need you."*

Presents ending in "ts" and presence ending in "ce" are not the same as John was to discover. Nothing he could give his wife—regardless of value—would ever mean as much to her as his presence.

Connecting with others in friendship is the best means of warding off loneliness as it is in relationships that we experience the comforting, reassuring, healing, qualities of presence.

Acceptance: The Acknowledging Quality of Presence

Acceptance is "quiet acknowledgment of what is." We share presence by acknowledging others as persons of worth and value without making a judgment of any kind (about what they do, say, think, feel, or wear), or requiring anything about them change. Presence comforts, reassures, and transforms the human spirit anytime one person says to another, "You don't have to do anything to be accepted by me. You are accepted, period!"

Valuing: The Assessing Quality of Presence

We share presence by valuing the fullness of the image of God in people. What we say by valuing others in this way is, "You are important quite apart from everyone else, from what you own, possess, or have access to. I value who you are, and all the things that make you who you are, your thoughts, feelings, ideas, experiences, attitudes and behaviors."

Relational aloneness is avoided anytime one person values the fullness of all that makes others who they are without condemning these things or asking they be changed.

Sharing: The Affirming Quality of Presence

We share presence by affirming the image of God in others. Relationships prosper and aloneness is avoided anytime a person permits another to share the fullness of who they are, "warts and all."

Sharing says, "I will withhold no part of myself from you nor surrender any part of myself to you. Nor will I require you to surrender any part of yourself to me. Sharing who we are, withholding no part of ourselves from each other, each of us remains our own person, separate, autonomous, and self-determining."

Commitment: The Cementing Quality of Presence

We share presence by committing ourselves to others. Commitment being love in action, relationships grow and prosper when by an act of the will individuals say to each other, "I am committed to meeting your needs and acting in your best interest in spite of how I feel."

Commitment understood as love in action accounts for the oneness in some relationships and the absence of oneness in others (married or single). In relationships where each person is committed to meeting the needs and acting in the best interest of the other, people are generally happy because the needs and interests of each person are given equal consideration.

With the passing of time, individuals committed to each other come to understand each other intuitively. Each senses what the other is thinking, discerns intuitively what the other is feeling, and with uncanny accuracy anticipates what the response of the other will be in a given situation.

Relationships characterized by commitment are remarkably free of game playing, a tactic whose objective is to seek advantage or dominance. Playing games weakens relationships, thus contributing to their ineffectiveness and possible demise.

"Let the past be the past" is a cardinal rule of relationships in which people are committed to each other. Individuals who share presence have no need to know each other's history. The past is past. Even if it were possible for each person to know all there is to know about the other, and one or both persons had committed the entire catalog of sins, each would still feel the same, their commitment to each other as strong as ever.

Intimacy: The Expressive Quality of Presence

In *New Beginnings for Single-Parent Families*, I introduced twelve ways or avenues for experiencing intimacy and sharing presence in relationships.[13] Of the twelve, Physical, Emotional, and Spiritual Intimacy are most important for us.

Physical Intimacy is a particularly effective avenue for sharing presence, building relationship, and warding off loneliness because it allows two people to see, hear, talk to, and, if appropriate, touch each other.

"When you have listened to me so that I know I am accepted, and you touch me, or, perhaps, hug me without either of us recoiling in shock, surprise, or reading anything into the behavior, we have shared presence in a special way."

We also share presence through emotional intimacy or self-disclosure. Self-disclosure is what happens when I share the fullness of who I am aware that I risk rejection.

From experience, most of us can testify of the risk involved in permitting ourselves to be vulnerable to another individual, letting another person see who we are apart from such things as titles, status, position, and possessions that shield us from public scrutiny.

Father John Powell captured the essence of this risk in his book, *Why Am I Afraid to Tell You Who I Am*, when he said, *"But, if I tell you who I am, you might not like who I am, and it is all that I have."*[14]

A third avenue through which presence is shared effectively is the avenue of Spiritual Intimacy. Spiritual intimacy is sharing the fullness of one's thoughts on matters of ultimate importance without requiring others to agree.

"When I have shared how I feel about such matters as heaven, eternity, hell, creation, divorce, forgiveness, sin, tithing, baptism, and salvation, and you have accepted these as partially defining who I am without attempting to convert me to your point of view, we have shared presence in an unusual way and loneliness is avoided."

'He Leadeth Me Beside Still Waters'

Confident of the shepherd's love and care, the sheep declares, *"He leads me beside still water."* Shepherds know how important water is to the health and well-being of sheep, and they will go to any length to secure water for them to drink. As water plays such a vital role in the care and management of sheep, the significance of green pastures is far greater than of being places where sheep can feed.

Sheep rise just before dawn to graze. If the grass is wet, they stay fit on the water ingested in the process of grazing. Quite likely then, "still water" in the Psalm is dew on the grass and not a stream of flowing water.

Understood in this way, the meaning of the phrase, *"He leadeth me beside still water"* can be rendered, "He makes me lie down in green pastures where I find the still water of dew."

'He Restoreth My Soul, He Leadeth Me In Paths Of Righteousness.'

David writes of restoration from the perspective of a shepherd who knows what it means for sheep to wander from his flock.

In all likelihood, on more than one occasion as his flock passed under his rod at the end of the day, David discovered one of his sheep missing and he went in search of it immediately knowing the possibilities were good that the lost sheep was also cast down.

Quite often a sheep with a full coat will lie down in a depression in the ground and roll onto its back, its feet pointing toward the sky. In this position sheep are said to be "cast down" because they are helpless, completely at the mercy of their enemies. If shepherds are not alert to the possibility that one of their sheep is missing, and, in all likelihood, cast down, in time the sheep will die of natural causes or fall prey to predators.

David writes as well from the perspective of someone who, having departed from the path of righteousness, knew what it meant to be cast down in one's soul.

When human sheep wander from the path of right action (or righteousness) and are sapped of inner strength and vigor by the weight of their sins, their situation is similar to that of cast down sheep.

Two of Jesus' disciples—Peter and Judas—knew what meant to be cast down in their soul.

It was never Peter's intention to deny Christ. Without question, the Apostle whom Jesus had given the name, Peter, which means "rock," never thought himself capable of such a thing and had said so quite forcefully on the Mount of Olives.

"Even if I have to die with you, I will never disown [deny] you."

It was not until he heard the cock crow for the third time that Peter realized he had done the very thing he said he would never do. Feeling in his soul the full weight of his deed, Peter left the courtyard of the High Priest and wept bitterly.

Judas also knew what it was to be cast down in his soul. Unable to undo or void his act of betrayal and alienated from the company of the Apostles, Judas sought to return the thirty pieces of silver given him. When the authorities would not accept the money, Judas took his life.

◆   ◆   ◆

Its every need met, the sheep in the Psalm is unable to contain its joy. In light of the many demonstrations of the shepherd's love, the sheep concludes, *"Surely, goodness and mercy shall follow me all the days of my life and I shall dwell in the house [or flock] of the Lord forever."*

Notes For Shepherds

Because the figures of shepherd and sheep in the Shepherd's Psalm are so strong and clear, it has much to teach us. There is much we can learn from it.

First of all, it teaches the Lord is our shepherd in the same way He was shepherd of the Psalmist. We are sheep of God's flock. He has chosen us and bought us just as shepherds choose and buy their sheep. Our purchase price was the life of His Son.

Isn't that what Good Friday is all about? A contemporary song says, *"We are the reason that He gave His life."* An old gospel hymn declares, *"Jesus paid it all,"* and in a passage of unparalleled beauty, John writes, *"God so loved the world that He gave His only begotten Son that whosoever believeth in Him might not perish, but have everlasting life."* (John 3:16. KJV)

The Psalm also makes it quite clear that like David, each one of us is shepherd of some human flock, be it the congregation of a church, members of one's family, the staff of a business, or the faculty of a university.

Regrettably, the life Jesus came to bring members of the human flock is not enjoyed by everyone. It eludes many because they are hungry. Even in the most prosperous and productive land in the world the number of people who depend upon food pantries, soup kitchens, and other food distribution centers is astounding.

Fear prevents a significant segment of the human flock from living the abundant life. Violence is an area of grave concern in today's world because of its pervasiveness (or scope), (b) its randomness (or lack of motive or reason), and (c) its many forms.

In a report to the American Academy of Child Psychiatry, three child psychiatrists and a pediatrician warned, *"Today's children are growing up in a society in which violence is accepted as the American way of life."*[15]

Dr. Henry Work, Clinical Professor of George Washington and Georgetown Universities, spoke to the issue of violence on television. *"In spite of overwhelming evidence correlating television violence with aggression,"* he said, *"television continues to be as violent as ever."* Dr. Work went on to say, *"the average child will witness 13,000 real or simulated deaths and 101,000 violent episodes on television by high school graduation."*[16]

A second member of the panel, Dr. Diane H. Schetky, child psychiatrist and Associate Clinical Professor of Psychiatry at the Yale University Child Study Center, spoke on the relationship of guns and violence. *"Today guns cause 1,700 injuries per year...and they give children the message that killing people is fun, and violence is an acceptable means of resolving conflicts. Further, studies show that providing a child with a toy gun increases aggressive behavior."*[17]

The third panel member, Dr. Paul Dyment, pediatrician, and team physician for a boy's ice hockey team, cautioned that while participation in team sports is beneficial for a child's development, watching or participating in violence in team sports can be detrimental to the development of a child's character. *"It was once believed,"* he said, *"that sports violence was cathartic for spectators; after watching it, they would not need to be violent themselves. Recent studies, however, show the exact opposite is true. Viewing violence causes both children and adults to behave more violently."*[18]

To live abundantly, America must cease to ignore and rationalize the fact that violence is so internalized in family life that it is no longer recognized for what it is, so profitable commercially that the media disregards altogether findings linking violence with aggression because violence sells movies, videos, and television time, and so ingrained in the public mind that many refuse to acknowledge any relationship between guns and violence.

In short, violence has become a way of life and an accepted means of settling differences, prompting one foreign observer to remark, *"Murder belongs to the American way of life like Coca-Cola and hot dogs."*[19]

Shepherds must recognize abundant life evades many because there is tension between themselves and other members of the flock.

Shepherds of the ancient world recognized the importance of unity within the flock and they understood tension destroyed that unity. Therefore, when one member of the flock sought to establish dominance over others by abusing them, shepherds acted swiftly to discipline the troublemaker and restore calm. In this context it is worth noting that sheep who strive after status and dominance are generally unhappy, while those not seeking these things are the flock's more contented members.

Those who shepherd human sheep would do well to set as a priority in their work creating a *"sense of the flock."*

T.S. Eliot once remarked, *"Most of the trouble in the world [and one might add, the Church] is caused by people wanting to be important."* The desire of James and John to surpass the other apostles in excellence, worth, and authority (which would make them feel important) created so much tension within the Company of the Disciples that Jesus found it necessary to inform them that servanthood rather than status and prominence, was the key to greatness in the Kingdom of God. *"He who would be the greatest among you,"* Jesus said, *"would be servant of all."*

Wanting to be important, Christians disturb the sense of the flock and do untold harm to each other and the cause of Christ in the world, especially by the judgments they make.

It is interesting to note Scripture does not prohibit the making of judgments altogether because of the necessity of discerning good from evil, distinguishing that which is constructive from that which is destructive, and determining the best foundation upon which to build one's life.

What Scripture cautions against is making the kind of judgments that censure a person's character, judgments that create tension and disturb the sense of the flock because they censure the character of a person in the eyes of the congregation and the community at large.

Christians also disturb the unity of the flock by withdrawing fellowship from those with whom they differ theologically, failing to allow room for what some evangelical Christians refer to as "unity in diversity," and insisting others practice their piety according to a given understanding of the Bible.

A sense of the flock is disturbed anytime one person refuses another the right to interpret the Bible according to the dictates of their own conscience, when differences of interpretation are permitted to become issues of belief and grounds for withholding fellowship, and when stories of the Bible must always turn out the same way.

The difficulty with demanding that stories of the Bible turn out one way is that the challenge of the Spirit and the deepening of faith that comes in dialogue with the Word of God is lost, and tension within the Body of Christ is the result.

◆　　◆　　◆

A third thing the Twenty-Third Psalm teaches is that like sheep, humans wander from the "paths of righteousness" and find themselves cast down in their souls.

The editors of *The Interpreter's Bible* understand "paths of righteousness" as paths that lead sheep to the sheep fold, which is the home of the shepherd; therefore, the phrase is best translated, "He leadeth me in paths that lead home to the shepherd."[20]

Dorothy Thrupp acknowledged the inclination of human sheep to wander in her hymn, *"Come, Thou Fount Of Every Blessing."* She writes, *"Prone to wander, Lord, I feel it. Prone to leave the God I love. He, to res-*

cue me from danger interposed His precious blood. Oh, to grace, how great a debtor daily I'm constrained to be. May thy goodness like a fetter, bind my wandering heart to thee."

Recognizing the pace and demands of a post-modern society capable of pushing people beyond the limits of their flexibility, shepherds and congregations who take their shepherding seriously can ill afford to be indifferent or complaisant when members of the flock wander from the path of righteousness. Unless sought after and restored to the flock, those who get separated and are cast down in their souls may not find their way back to the Body of Christ.

Regrettably, far too often, human sheep wander from human flocks and no one discovers they are missing, thus, no one goes in search of them. Only shepherds and congregations whose goal is abundant life for all members of the flock are likely to go in search of those who have gotten separated, and restore with grace, those who are cast down.

2

Oh the Blessedness
of the Good Shepherd

Because the figures of shepherd and sheep are so well defined and
the relationship of shepherd and sheep such an intimate one, the
Shepherd's Psalm has an air of timeless relevance about it.

We identify easily with the sheep because in many ways we are like
it. To lie down, we require the same things it requires, namely, freedom from hunger, tension, fear, and aggravation.

Identifying with the shepherd, however, is another matter altogether, as few of us are sufficiently confident and secure in who we are
to consistently and selflessly put the needs and concerns of others
ahead of our own as shepherds must do if sheep in their care are to say,
"I shall not want."

◆　　　◆　　　◆

Jesus understood Himself to be a shepherd. Human sheep were the
reason for His coming. *"I have come that they* [meaning members of the
human flock] *might have life and have it to the full [abundantly]."* (KJV,
John 10:10)

While Jesus did not elaborate upon what He meant by abundant
life, as a shepherd He would have had in mind a quality of life in which
members of His flock had everything they need.

With Christ as our model and the life of the sheep of Psalm Twenty-Three a paradigm of the abundant life, what will be required of shepherds if human sheep are to know the life He came to bring?

◆   ◆   ◆

If human sheep are to experience the abundant life Jesus came to bring, those who lead them must know themselves "called" to the vocation of shepherd.

In the Introduction to *The Call*, W. Brugh Joy describes the call of God as "*...a revelation, an inner prompting, a vision, causing an individual to turn from a personal, self-centered, and superficially expressed life to that of a servant of the divine.*"[1]

Originally, to be called meant "to be addressed by a voice." As it is God who addresses men and women, all callings are religious. It is the understanding that they have been called that lends dignity and authenticity to the vocation of shepherd and brings significance to their work.

In the same passage in which Jesus speaks of Himself as the Good Shepherd, He contrasts the dedication of persons called to the vocation of shepherd with that of individuals hired to tend sheep.

As a general rule, individuals who hire themselves out to others do not bring the same level of commitment to the task [be it tending sheep or repairing VCRs] as those for whom tending sheep or repairing VCRs is a calling.

Only the most conscientious person hired to tend sheep was likely to exhibit the same level of dedication as the shepherd.

Lacking the dedication of shepherds, when predators were about, hirelings were likely to place their personal safety ahead of the sheep and leave them unattended, whereas, shepherds would ignore their personal safety, place themselves between the sheep and whatever threatened them, and, if required, give their life in their defense.

If human sheep are to know abundant life those who lead them must be convinced they have been called to the vocation of shepherd as only those confident of their calling are likely to commit themselves to meeting the needs and acting in their best interest of sheep in their care.

In *New Beginnings for Single-Parent Families*, I defined human "need" as *"...something that cannot go unmet for very long, which cannot be ignored for an extended period without an individual experiencing a loss of self respect, self-esteem, and well-being."*[2]

In that same work, "concern" was defined as *"something that occupies our attention; something we think about and discuss with others; yet, may or may not act upon."*[3]

Whereas, one would think the needs and concerns of people in a super-technological society would differ from those of persons in other societies, in reality they do not. In any society, there are eight items that constitute needs or concerns for people:

- Self worth or self esteem
- Acceptance
- Relationships
- Loneliness
- Sex and Sexuality
- Finances
- Assistance with children, and
- Knowing the Will and Purpose of God.

Self Worth As Need and Concern

Self worth is a need and a concern in every age. We carry a mental image of who we are in our mind. Because this image functions as a frame of reference through which we process the world, it has a bearing upon everything we do, say, think, and feel.

Some aspects of the image we have of ourselves make us attractive to others. They draw people to us while other aspects tend to hold people at a distance, perhaps, even drive them away. Some facets ease communication between ourselves and others while other facets complicate and clog the communication process. Some aspects help us manage conflict effectively, thus minimizing the possibility of conflict becoming a destructive force in relationships, while other aspects sow seeds of friction, strife, and discord.

◆   ◆   ◆

As the vocation of shepherd is a calling to a high level of involvement in the lives of people, it is essential that shepherds be convinced of their worth and value if they are to act selflessly in the interests of human sheep, and, at the same time, withstand forces that would push them beyond the limits of their flexibility, separate them from the core of their being, and render them vulnerable to burnout.

Lacking inner confidence and security, shepherds are as likely as members of their flocks to succumb to burnout.[4]

Burnout renders shepherds less effective, less potent, and less selfless in their service. They cease putting the needs of others ahead of their own. They detach from the very people they are called to serve because the power and delight of being a servant (the very thing that makes one great in the Kingdom of God) is lost as burnout progresses.

◆   ◆   ◆

Not only is it important that shepherds be convinced they are persons of worth and value, it is essential that they recognize their personal worth and value lies in who they are rather than in what they do. While shepherds have every right to esteem themselves, they must avoid the seductive notion that personal worth and value stem from or is enhanced by what they do as this kind of thinking is self-glorification.

Self-glorification is thinking, "I am important because I practice law or medicine or play a professional sport." It is loving oneself for the wrong reason, and encouraging others to do the same. It is seeing oneself in the wrong light and encouraging others to see you that way. Where worth and value are concerned, "who people are" is more important than "what people do."

The Psalmist raises the issue of human worth and value in Psalm Eight when he asks, *"What is man [What is his worth and value] that you are mindful of him, the son of man that you care for him?"*

Verses later, in awe of the beauty, majesty, and wonder about him, he declares man's worth and value beyond measure, proof of which is seen in the fact that God has *"created [man] just a little lower than the heavenly beings and crowned him with glory and honor."*

The glory and honor with which humankind has been crowned is the honor of reflecting the image of the God in whose likeness we are created.

Humans glorify God by reflecting who He is. To the extent that the image we present to the world reflects the image of the One who has created us, we glorify Him.

◆   ◆   ◆

Not only must shepherds be inwardly confident and secure in themselves to withstand forces that would render them vulnerable to burnout, to remain true to their calling they must develop the capacity to live independent of the good opinion of others.

Called by God, shepherds, like parents, are sometimes in a better position to know what is best for sheep in their care than are sheep themselves.

Regrettably, members of the human flock are seldom aware of what is involved in the care and management of human sheep, much less what is required to be a good shepherd. And, as human sheep are seldom as trusting as their animal counterparts, should the shepherd's proclamation touch a sensitive area, likely as not, they forget he is acting in their best interests.

Yet, to fulfill their calling, shepherds must say and do things that are in the best interests of sheep in spite of the fact that sheep may not appreciate what is done.

While we all desire to be well thought of (and certainly shepherds want the approval of members of their flocks), in order to be the instrument they are called to be, shepherds must develop the capacity of living independent of the good opinion of others. Shepherds unable to live in this way tend to become obsequious and fawning in their relationships, or they relax in their efforts at meeting the needs and acting in the best interests of all members of their flock.

Acceptance As Need and Concern

Acceptance, like self worth, is a need and a concern in any age. We accept others by quietly acknowledging them as creatures made in the image of God without making a judgment of any kind (about what they do, say, think, or feel), or requiring them to change in any way.

Acceptance is acknowledging the twig is already bent. And while one might prefer the twig bent in another direction, requiring others to change accomplishes nothing apart from rendering acceptance invalid.

Relationship As Need and Concern

Relationship or relatedness is also a need and concern of people in every age—so important to the abundant life that in the mind of psychologist James Kennedy "relationships are life."[5]

Relatedness is man's basic need. In the Garden of Eden, the Lord saw *"it was not good for the man to be [or live] alone,"* so He created Eve to fulfill Adam's need.

In a society fueled by technology, opportunities for connecting with others for the purpose of building friendships diminish with each technological advance.

As opportunities for connecting with others diminish, it becomes increasingly rare to have one person with whom one can share their innermost self, as it takes time and energy to build the kind of relationship in which people feel comfortable sharing information about themselves that is not only privileged but unavailable by other means. Those fortunate enough to have someone in their life with whom they can share their innermost being find life becomes a garden as Goethe said.

In the decades ahead, relationships are destined to continue an area of concern for Society and the Church. The Church must structure services of worship and develop ministries that provide opportunities for connecting in friendship.

Sexuality As Need and Concern

Sexuality is also an area of need and concern in every age. Sexuality is an expression of human personality. As such neither pleasure nor procreation exhausts its meaning nor reveals its full scope.

As the Twenty-First Century dawns, however, sexuality is an area laden with difficulties.

In part, difficulties in this area are ours because in the process of making the transition from an industrial to a post-modern society, Americans have let go, lost, or left behind a number of important beliefs, traditions, practices, and principles once relied upon as guidelines of behavior.

In the absence of these stabilizing influences significant changes have occurred in this important area of life.

To begin, sex has been removed from the context of sexuality and defined as a need. Defining sex as a need has led to more confusion than one would suppose, primarily because sex is not a need. It is a desire.

Defining sex as a need leads inevitably to (a) the rationalizing of sexual activity as meeting a need, (b) the supposition that the physical side of sex (bios) can be isolated from and viewed as autonomous of the spirit (pneuma), and (c) the equating of sexual activity with intimacy.

Theologian Wayne Oates challenges the belief that the physical side of sex can be isolated from and viewed as autonomous of the spirit on the basis of the biblical understanding that body and spirit are a unity.

Each is part of and each affects the other. Neither can be separated from nor function apart from the other. As the biological side of sex is not autonomous of the spirit, it is impossible to have purely physical sex.[6]

It was Abraham Maslow who thought of needs as gaps between a present condition and a desired or prescribed condition. The desire for intimacy is really a gap between the present condition of a relationship and what people want to experience in their relationships.[7] Equating sex with intimacy leads people to suppose this gap can be filled with sexual activity.

What we are finding is that while people are free to do what they like with regard to sex, *"No age has enjoyed sex less than this one."*[8]

Finance As Need and Concern

Finance is another area of need and/or concern certain to occupy society and its people in the current century.

Our welfare system and the present debate over welfare and welfare reform speak volumes on finances as an area of need and concern for all families.

In particular, finances are cause for concern in single-parent families, and while alimony and child support are issues normally addressed in decrees of divorce and separation, a significant portion of the monies assigned in these instruments are not paid. This helps account for the presence of fifty percent of single-parent mothers in the work force.

Because finances are also an area of need and concern among nuclear families, the number of women at work outside the home has grown steadily since World War II.

At the present rate women are entering the work force, it is anticipated that sometime in the first quarter of the Twenty-First Century eighty-five percent of all women in their prime childbearing and child-rearing years will be at work outside the home.[9]

Assistance with Children As Need and Concern

With so many women employed outside the home, assistance with children is destined to be an area of critical need and concern of parents in the immediate future.

Small businesses, giant corporations (such as IBM and ABC), as well as the Federal Government have implemented programs to help parents meet family responsibilities. These programs range from unpaid family leave, to providing quality day care in centers associated with the work place, to flextime that allows women to work hours compatible with the needs of their families. Some mothers take their children to work with them as did Joan Lunden of ABC's *"Good Morning America,"* when she returned to work following the birth of her daughter.

Knowing the Will of God As Need and Concern

In any age, knowing the Will and Purpose of God is the most personal, and, perhaps, most bewildering of the eight needs and concerns of people.

Confusion in this area is usually the result of viewing and using God's Will and His Purpose (His Intention) as interchangeable terms, when they are not.

God's Will is the function of His being which He uses to determine Intention or Purpose. Therefore, It is quite possible that when people say, "I want to know God's Will," what they are really saying is, "I want to know God's Intention or Purpose for my life."

While people desire to know God's Purpose, they are desperate to understand how to discern His Purpose.

The not-so-obvious answer is, "God communicates His Intention using faculties with which He has endowed humankind, faculties of mind, will, emotion, imagination, and memory."

John Powell refers to these faculties as the "antennae" of our listening.[10]

God puts His ideas, perspectives, thoughts, desires, and vision directly into the human mind.

He touches human emotions to bring peace, comfort, and assurance to human sheep, rearrange their priorities, and sensitize them to the needs of those about us.

He introduces His words, vision, and possibilities directly into the human imagination. He communicates through memories stored in the mind, stirring up memories needed to help us avoid repeating mistakes made previously.[11]

Discerning God's Communication

Being certain it is God who communicates with us has always been a troublesome issue as humans can, and often do, simulate the voice of God. Individuals will testify in glowing terms one moment how God is speaking to them or working in their lives only to question a moment later whether it was His speaking, or their own simulation of His speaking.

So, if we are to know God's Purpose and Intention, how are we to discern whether the voice communicating intention and purpose to us is that of God or our simulation of His voice?

God's Communication Does Not Fade

We can know it is God communicating with us when the message does not fade with the passing of time. As what we know becomes a part of us, when God communicates His Purpose, that communication becomes a part of us. It does not dim with the passing of time. It remains clear and strong, deepening our awareness and appreciation of the world around us, making us more loving.[12]

God's Communication Changes Human Perspective

When God communicates His Purpose, it changes our perspective of Him, the world, and people. We see God as He is. Majestic. High. Lifted up. We see ourselves as God sees us. Separate. Unique. Special. We see others as God sees them. Unique. Separate. Special.

God's Communication Motivates Us to Love and Service

When God communicates His Intention, we become more loving, more open to serving others. He reveals the direction of our service by endowing us with the tools we need to carry it out. His Purpose is related to the manner in which He has gifted us.

As we progress through life, we acquire special abilities and skills through hard work and dedication.

The motivation for developing the talents given us, and honing abilities acquired is knowing that, on some level, what we do not only adds to our well-being and that of others, but also advances God's Purposes in the world.

◆   ◆   ◆

It is essential that shepherds recognize how important the needs and/or concerns mentioned (or combinations thereof) are to the health and well-being of human sheep as anything short of optimum health in the area of the spirit diminishes their capacity to share presence in ways that comfort, transform, reassure, and heal.

Matthew demonstrates Jesus' sensitivity to the well-being of the human spirit in a section of his gospel (Matthew 6:19-7:12) in which he has gathered a number of teachings pertaining to the religious life. Included among these is the exhortation to, *"Lay up for yourselves treasure in heaven."*

Jesus taught we are not to be troubled in spirit concerning the basic necessities of life. *"Take no thought for your life,"* (reads the King James) *"Don't be anxious,"* (says the Revised Standard Version) *"about what ye shall eat, or what ye shall drink; nor yet for your body, what ye shall put on."*

Scripture affirms our Heavenly Father knows we have need of life's basic necessities. He knows we cannot do without such things as food, clothing, and shelter for an extended period without suffering a loss of self-esteem, self-respect, and well-being.

He knows as well how difficult it is to entertain thoughts of an abundant life when one is hungry, homeless, and inadequately clothed.

Of course, when Jesus said, "Don't be anxious", He was not advocating withdrawing from life or denouncing the world. And in telling us, "Don't worry about things," He was not suggesting that we adopt a naive, indifferent stance toward life. Nor was He attempting to relieve us of the responsibility of doing everything in our power (using the talents with which we have been endowed and the skills acquired) to provide the necessities of food, clothing, and shelter for ourselves, our families, and others for whom we are responsible.

What Jesus is saying is, 'Don't engage in the kind of thinking that disturbs, distracts, or troubles your spirit because the One who gives you life will also provide for you."

Psychology supports the view that anxious thinking disturbs the mind, disrupts the personality, and troubles the spirit. Another result of this kind of thinking is it leads to divided loyalties and attempts at serving two masters, something Jesus instructs us not to do. A life of abundance is impossible when loyalties are divided.

What the Good Shepherd is saying to human sheep is, "Don't worry about anything to the point that it disturbs your peace of mind. Anxious, overly concerned, worrisome thinking doesn't add a single moment to life. It does, in fact, shorten it. So, rather than engaging in this type of thinking, focus your attention upon seeking the Kingdom of God, confident that the Master of that Kingdom will add unto you what life requires you to have."

So, the message of the Good Shepherd in John Ten can be summed up like this, "I have come to bring life characterized by abundance rather than concern. Because I am your shepherd and you my sheep, I will see that you have the things you need. Meanwhile, my word to you is, 'Don't be anxious or troubled concerning the things of your life.' Your Heavenly Father knows you have need of these things."

Notes For Shepherds

If sheep are to experience abundant life in the Twenty-First Century, shepherds must model themselves after the Good Shepherd. This means, among other things, identifying with Him and imitating Him in daily life.

Identification is an emotional process. It is our human way of declaring, "I want to be like you."

Identifying with Christ, shepherds intentionally think the thoughts of God because His thoughts are higher than theirs.

Thinking the thoughts of God, the feelings of shepherds toward sheep in their care become increasingly those of the Good Shepherd for His sheep.

As their thoughts and feelings become more and more those of the Good Shepherd, shepherds imitate Him in the behavioral aspects of their lives, consistently doing what is required that sheep in their care might have abundant life.

◆   ◆   ◆

Undoubtedly, the role of shepherd will be as demanding in the future as it is today. One of the issues certain to vex shepherds is that so many members of the human flock cannot enjoy abundant life because they are hungry, homeless, or poorly clothed.

Fear in the lives of human sheep is another issue certain to dominate the thinking of shepherds.

Shepherds must never underestimate the value of their presence as a force in the lives of fearful people. Presence is a gift to be given, no strings attached, nothing expected in return.

Offered under these conditions, presence becomes a gift of love, the kind of love that "casts out fear" because there are no conditions to be met to receive it, no barriers to its enjoyment, no reason to anticipate rejection.

◆   ◆   ◆

Tension between members of the human flock will also require the attention of shepherds.

By the very nature of their role, shepherds are peacemakers. Shepherds work for peace by making themselves available to individuals struggling to resolve interpersonal differences when they could as easily excuse themselves with an "I'm too busy" or "It's not my problem." Perhaps it is their willingness "not to be busy" and their willingness to address a problem that is not their own that earns peacemakers the honor of being called "Sons of God."

Here's a valuable relational truth for shepherds of human sheep. Just as that sense of who we are—identity—is formed in the context of relationships, in one way or another, everyone we meet tells us something about who we are and about our relationship with God.

If shepherds will remain alert to the fact that everyone they meet is telling them something, and muster the grace to consider what people are telling them, that information can be quite helpful in the exercise of their calling.

Another issue shepherds are certain to encounter is that in the relationships they establish with members of their flocks are factors that not only limit success, but which, if ignored are capable of stretching shepherds beyond their limits, rendering them susceptible to compassion fatigue.

The Nature Of Caring Relationships

Shepherds establish caring relationships because human sheep have problems. Each day one or more members of the flock come bringing a host of reminders of human frailty.

To maintain their effectiveness, it is essential that shepherds understand the very things that motivate people to establish caring relationships also work to limit their success.

For example, those who give and those who receive care tend to view what happens and to evaluate results (or lack of results) from different perspectives. To the recipient whatever creates the need for a caring relationship may seem like "the end of the world," or at a minimum, a "grave emergency," while to the shepherd it is "old hat," "mundane," "routine," "the same old thing," because he or she has seen it before, perhaps, the same day.

Often overlooked is the reality that caring relationships involve the expenditure of enormous amounts of energy, and while human sheep are long on soaking up the energy of shepherds they tend to be short on showing appreciation for it, as caring is "what shepherds do."

The difficulty with regard to the expenditure of energy lies in the fact that when energy in the tank of the shepherd runs low they run the risk of succumbing to "compassion fatigue," the name by which burnout is known among care givers.

Shepherds must be prepared to cope with the fact that caring relationships end when the problems of human sheep have been dealt with satisfactorily. More often than shepherds care to admit, and much to their dismay, far too often in the wake of having struggled long and hard with member(s) of their flock, these people remove their membership to another church.

For these and other reasons as well, it seems likely that many whom God would call to the vocation of shepherd will not respond affirmatively because for them the cost of caring on a daily basis is too high. Many will ignore the call of God because they fear the pace, stress, and demands of caring for others may stretch them beyond their limits. And some are forced to recognize theirs is not the heart of a shepherd.

Others will shun the vocation of the shepherd because they recognize that they are not sufficiently confident and secure in themselves to meet the needs and act in the best interests of others in anything resembling a potent manner.

A great number of people will refuse the high calling of the shepherd because they are unable to grasp the paradox that "giving is receiving." Maria made this point in *The Sound of Music* when she sang, *"Love isn't love til you give it away."* Desiring a deeper, fuller identity with sheep in his care, the shepherd gives away his love knowing it will return like bread cast upon the waters.

With Chapter Three, our focus shifts to the Beatitudes of Matthew and Luke in which are found traits and characteristics of the ideal disciple and citizen of the Kingdom of God. The goal of all who would be good shepherds is to exhibit the traits and characteristics of the ideal disciple found in the Beatitudes.

3

Oh the Blessedness of Those Who Are Poor in Spirit

◆

The Beatitude of Trust

The Sermon on the Mount (Matthew 5-7) is generally regarded as the essence of all Jesus taught in His earthly ministry. Matthew sets the scene for Christ's Sermon in two sentences, *"Now when he saw the crowds, he went up on a mountainside and sat down. His disciples came to him, and he began to teach them..."*

In the time of Jesus to be a disciple meant more than simply being an adherent, a pupil, or a learner. It involved identifying with a teacher, pledging one's loyalty to him, and accepting his teachings as the rule for one's life.

Having assumed the position of a teacher, Jesus *"...opened his mouth and taught them."* Though used sparingly, when this phrase appears the reader can anticipate something of great importance is about to happen, that the speaker regards what he is about to say as extremely important, and, on occasion, that the purpose for offering a particular teaching is to impact the lives of those with whom a teacher has formed a close relationship.

Jesus delivered The Beatitudes in Aramaic, the kind of Hebrew spoken by Jews of the First Century. To communicate the blessings Jesus intended to bestow upon men, Matthew and Luke introduce them using the Greek word *makarios* (blessed) because it articulates a state of

45

well-being or blessedness in which people enjoy the favor of God and experience the happiness Jesus had in mind for members of the human flock.[1]

Happiness in the Beatitudes differs markedly from happiness as contemporary society understands it. In the Beatitudes happiness is a state of well-being characterized by wholeness, contentment, tranquility, fulfillment, and peace, while in contemporary society it is essentially an externally induced state dependent upon chance, luck, accident, or circumstance.[2]

We see evidence of this understanding of happiness in the antics and boisterous outcries of game show contestants upon whom luck smiles giving them a chance to win large sums of money or prizes, in the zeal with which Americans enter contests requiring nothing beyond the ability to enter personal information on coupons, and in the haste with which people drop their names in boxes labeled "Win a prize" at fairs, expos, and club gatherings.

As much as anything, however, the essence of Beatitudinal happiness is peace.

On the Thursday prior to His death, Jesus ate His last meal with the disciples. After Judas' departure on his mission of betrayal, Jesus informs the disciples that He will be with them for just a short while.

The disciples are understandably dejected at the thought of Jesus' leaving them. Knowing His death will substantially change the meaning of their lives, Jesus speaks words of reassurance to them. *"I will not leave you comfortless...Peace I leave with you, my peace I give unto you: not as the world giveth, give I unto you."* (John 14:27)

The word used in this passage for peace is *eirana*. It identifies the peace Jesus gives as inner peace, peace independent of outside conditions because it is dependent upon who God is.

If it were possible to blend together blessings to be bestowed upon those who embody the traits and characteristics identified in the Beatitudes and the peace Jesus left His disciples, the result would be a state of inner tranquility, wholeness, favor, and happiness described by Matthew as "blessedness."[3]

"Oh, the blessedness of those who are poor in spirit, pure in heart, meek, merciful; those who mourn; those who work for peace; those who hunger and thirst after righteousness; those who are persecuted for righteousness' sake, or have all manner of evil said against them for God's sake, for they shall bask in the favor of God and know inner peace, tranquility, and happiness."

Jesus spoke the Beatitudes as declaratory statements. Accordingly, the First Beatitude is understood as saying, *"Oh the blessedness of the man who is poor in spirit, for his is the Kingdom of God."*

To appreciate the thrust of what Jesus was had in mind when He spoke of being poor in spirit requires exploring the meaning of "poor" and "spirit".

The New Testament recognizes two classes of poor. The first of these, the *penes*, or working class poor, are mentioned only once. (2 Corinthians 9:9) The penes made a living with their hands, and while they were not destitute, pay received for their labor was seldom enough to enable them to rise to a level at which they were no longer considered poor.[4]

The primary word for poor in the New Testament—the word that appears in the First Beatitude—is *ptochoi*. It appears thirty-four times, each time describing persons living in abject poverty; helpless, destitute, beaten down, often reduced to begging as a means of survival. For this reason, the singular of ptochoi *(ptochos)* is often translated "beggar."[5]

If living in abject poverty was not enough, the poor in the First Beatitude were without standing and influence in the community and lacking in education. In short, they were people mired in conditions that drain the human spirit making it difficult for men to trust.

In Biblical times, the Law provided some relief to the poor by granting them produce of the land in Sabbatical years, allowing them to glean harvested fields, dismissing their debts in the Year of Jubilee, and collecting alms for them in services of the synagogue. Nonetheless, the ptochoi lived at a level at which people have nothing.[6]

◆   ◆   ◆

Having identified the poor in the Beatitude, what does it mean to be poor in spirit? And why are men blessed because they are poor in this way?

Scripture champions the belief that we are spiritual beings because we are created in the image of God, who Himself, is Spirit.

Spirit is the essence of life in man. It is the source of the power and energy required for human living as well as the seat of humankind's higher mental and moral life.[7]

To create man in His own image, God first made a form. The form was incomplete, however, because it was without life.

So God imparted life to the form by breathing His Spirit into it. Animated and energized by the life-giving breath of God the form became a living "being" or "soul" capable of reflecting the image of God.

Spirit is the incorporeal dimension of the image of God in human-kind. It is that aspect of our being that recognizes and resonates to things divine and eternal, enabling us to know and commune with God.

Martin Luther spoke of Spirit as the *"highest and noblest part of man, which qualifies him to lay hold of incomprehensible, invisible, eternal things; in short, it is the house where Faith and God's word are at home."*[8]

This highest and noblest part of man is the dimension of our being in which true worship—worship in which human spirit is aligned with God's Spirit—takes place. As *"God is Spirit...they who worship Him must worship in spirit and in truth."* (John 4:24)

Spirit is also that dimension of being at which one person "knows" another. The only way one person can really "know" another is by con-necting spirit-to-spirit with that person, and individuals know each other in the deepest sense only when connected in this way. It is this fact that differentiates sexual intercourse between people committed to each other from simply having sex. When Scripture says Abraham knew his wife, it is describing more than the physical coming together of Abraham and Sarah. It is documenting the connecting of their spirits.

◆　　◆　　◆

When Jesus declared His Intention to bless the poor in spirit, His immediate focus was on people about Him, many of whom were vitally concerned about the basic necessities of life.

Yet, His instructions were, *"Do not worry [Take no thought]" (KJV)" Don't be anxious,"* (RSV), *"about your life, what you will eat or drink; or about your body, what you will wear [things that concerned the poor the most]."*

James spoke to the issue of refusing to worry and be anxious as a trial or testing of faith. As poverty is not a desired state and Scripture does not suggest there is virtue in being poor, what James is saying to the poor of the First Beatitude is, rejoice "in" the circumstance of poverty, not because of it. "In your poverty," says James, "don't be anxious. Don't worry. Instead, rejoice."

We rejoice "in" poverty or in any circumstance of life for that matter, because it is in the circumstances of our lives that God works for good. And while there is no virtue in being poor, for some to become poor in spirit means detaching from concern for the necessities of life and trusting in God to provide.

So, the poverty blessed in the First Beatitude is not poverty that reflects a lack of anything, be it influence, possessions, standing, or food, clothing, and shelter. The poverty blessed is poverty of spirit, a state of being created by detaching from things of earth and placing one's trust in God.

When Jesus said, *"Take no thought for the morrow, what ye shall eat, or what ye shall drink, or what ye shall wear,"* He was not suggesting men cease responsible thinking. His reason for saying, *"Take no thought (about the basic necessities of life)"* was to remove from the minds of men concern for things promised them by God. Taking no thought—refusing to be anxious—about such things as food, clothing, and shelter is detaching from things of earth in the interest of becoming the kind of person whom God would bless.

While for some becoming poor in spirit means detaching from concern for the basic necessities of life, for others it means detaching from wealth, possessions, status, position and placing one's trust in God.

In the final analysis the challenge of the First Beatitude is the same for rich or poor. "To become poor in spirit you must detach from earth and things of earth and place your trust in God."

Detaching from things of earth—for rich or poor—is simply removing the circumstance of one's life as a hindrance to spiritual growth. Detaching is removing anything that deters one from pursuing what is really important, namely, the Kingdom of God.

Detaching from things of earth is certain to be an issue for Americans as they move through the Twenty-First Century because possessions and wealth bring status, prominence, and influence in contemporary society and nations of the world. However, as long as men and women are attached to such things, that state of spiritual trust and reliance recognized as "poor in spirit" will not be theirs.

The paradoxical thing about the poor in spirit is, whether poor or rich, they are blessed because they have discovered the way to inner peace, wholeness, contentment, and happiness lies in detaching from things of earth and trusting in God.

Most biblical scholars consider the Kingdom of Heaven to be the dominant theme of Jesus' teaching about Himself (what kind of King He knew Himself to be and the kind of Kingdom He came to bring). Matthew speaks almost exclusively of the Kingdom of Heaven while Luke and Mark speak of the Kingdom of God. The two phrases point to the same reality, a spiritual community in which men seek to do the Will of God as perfectly on earth as it is in heaven.

Jesus Himself had these things to say about this Kingdom:

"My Kingdom is not of this world." (John 18:36)

"Ye cannot see the Kingdom of God." (John 3:3)

"It does not come with observation." (Luke 17:20)

"The Kingdom of Heaven is at hand." (Matthew 3:2)

"The Kingdom of God has come." (Matthew 12:28)

"The Kingdom of Heaven is among you." (John 18:36)

"Kingdom of Heaven is within you." (Luke17:12).

From what Jesus has to say, it seems clear that the Kingdom He came to bring is not a kingdom in the usual sense. It is a spiritual rather than physical kingdom "at hand, among men, and within men." As such it has no capital building, no legislative body, no treasury, no judiciary, and no standing army, issues no currency, collects no taxes, and passes no laws.

Peace, happiness, and joy are visible expressions of that Kingdom in the lives of the poor in spirit as things of earth no longer control them or dominate their thinking. Trusting in God to meet their needs they focus upon doing the will of God on earth in the same way it is done in heaven. For this, they are blessed with God's favor.

Notes For Shepherds

It seems reasonable to assume the pace and demands of life in the century ahead will continue to escalate—for shepherd and sheep alike—placing additional stress and strain upon each.

To be effective in the care and management of human sheep, shepherds must build interpersonal trust with people already pushed to the limits of their flexibility by forces of change and transition.

Trust is what happens when the exterior of an individual speaks the same truth as their interior, when what one knows himself to be on the inside squares with how one lives out that truth in view of the world.

For human sheep to trust a shepherd, they must be able to rely upon his (or her) word and deed. If a shepherd says to a member of his flock, "I will meet you on the observation deck of the Empire State Building—or anywhere else—at six a.m.," and that person chooses to check, they have a right to expect the shepherd will be there.

When, in the care and management of human sheep, shepherds prove themselves consistent in word and deed, they will be trusted.

Communication also plays an important role in the development or erosion of trust between shepherds and sheep in their care. Shepherds must say what they mean and mean what they say. Their "Yea" must mean "Yea," and their "Nay" mean "Nay."

They must be willing to share matters of importance and mutual concern with members of their flocks. It is difficult for human sheep to trust shepherds unwilling to share their thoughts, ideas, opinions, feelings, and experiences, shepherds unwilling to level with them, shepherds who seek to elevate themselves above the people they are supposed to serve.

And nothing undermines trust more completely than for human sheep to detect the shepherd has hidden agendas where they are concerned. Hidden agendas lead sheep to feel manipulated and controlled.

◆   ◆   ◆

To be trusted, shepherds must demonstrate expertise. Human sheep want their shepherds to know what they are doing and what they are talking about. To achieve a level of expertise needed to build trust shepherds must take advantage of every opportunity available for enhancing their ability to lead and demonstrate expertise.

In some instances leadership is learned and expertise acquired by reading, listening to tapes, attending conferences and seminars, or watching videos regarding situations reflected in the lives of members of one's flock.

Shepherds must also be honest enough to recognize when they have come to the limit of their understanding and refuse the temptation of falling back on that awkward, but revealing response, "Have faith," which in most instances, simply means, "I don't know."

As shepherds function as change agents in the lives of human sheep, they are more likely to be trusted when they are actively involved in the lives of people, vitally interested in what happens to them, excited about the possibilities of their lives, and willing to walk with them through their Valleys of Dark Shadows.

While displaying care and concern for human sheep, shepherds must also exercise caution lest they ignore or disregard their own needs or permit the requirements and demands of service to push them beyond their limits. To do so is to court burnout and risk becoming ineffective in one's calling.

Called to be a shepherd in the Twenty-First Century, ask yourself,

"What must I do if the sheep in my care are to experience abundant life?"

"What will be required of me if members of my flock are to lie down free of fear, hunger, tension, and aggravation?"

"What will be asked of me if the sheep in my care are to declare, 'I have everything' I need?"

This much can be said with certainty. Shepherds who are poor in spirit, who place their complete trust in God, will be blessed, for theirs is the Kingdom of Heaven.

4

Oh the Blessedness
of Those Who Mourn

❖

The Beatitude of Compassion

Following the death of his wife, Vance Havener published a rare
and candid account of personal grief titled, *Though I Walk
Through the Valley*. Deeply involved in the process of adjusting to the
loss of his marital partner, this respected clergyman concluded there are
three types of days, each unique in character and purpose.

First, there are "Mountaintop Days," days when one's mood is
upbeat, confident, enthusiastic, and outgoing. People are happy with
themselves. They feel successful. Relationships are rewarding. Things
go well. Life is fulfilling.

It is not the lot of humankind to dwell indefinitely on the moun-
taintops of life, however, as life, like "Ole Man River" just keeps rolling
along.

Accordingly, days filled with optimism, confidence, and enthusiasm
run their course and in their wake come life's Ordinary Days during
which individuals function as if in neutral, contacts with others neither
energizing nor depressing them, conversation seldom getting beyond,
"Good morning, how are you?"

During Ordinary Days, people approach whatever work there is to
be done in a frame of mind akin to that of Sir Edmund Hillary who,

when asked why he wanted to climb Mount Everest, replied, *"Because it's there."*

And then it happens! Ordinary days pass and, likely as not, in their wake come a succession of Valley Days in which one's energy level is low, one's mood subdued, and more often than not, people must contend with doubt, disappointment, tedium, discouragement, failure, and loss.

While we skip through Mountaintop Days and plod through Ordinary Days, we trudge through the Valley Days of life.

On the surface, a strong case could be made for assuming Jesus spoke the Second Beatitude with Valley Days in mind. Taking a literal approach, the Second Beatitude could be understood as saying, "Blessed are those who endure life's difficult, disintegrating, and discouraging experiences, for they shall be comforted."

Focusing on the unique character and purpose of Mountaintop, Ordinary, and Valley days, one discovers realities that have a bearing upon the Second Beatitude. The first of these acknowledges life is much the same for all of us, the second affirms everyone has the same range of experience, and the third declares life seldom remains the save for very long.

In moving between extremes of birth and death, life is much the same for us all. It twists and turns forcing us to veer left and at other times right of the course we had thought to follow.

Occasionally, in the same way an earthquake changes the course of a river, experiences of loss compel us to make significant departures from the path we had thought to take.

Then, as if life needed additional complications, the pace of life tends to vary. When we are enjoying ourselves or deeply involved in creating something, life flies by. When discouraged or disappointed, when we have failed at something or have experienced loss, the pace of life slows considerably, sometimes coming to a halt.

Perhaps, the figure that best brings these observations together is that of a roller coaster. "Life is like a roller coaster" in that it is constantly in motion, has its ups and downs, its curves and its straight-a-ways, and is continually changing speed and direction.

These observations point to the obvious, namely, that each one of us is destined to walk through the Valley of Dark Shadows from time to time because

- People are certain to disappoint us

- People break commitments to us

- People betray our friendship and trust

- People refuse to help in times of need, and

- Persons emotionally significant to us are going to die.

Fortunately, psychology can help us understand what Jesus had in mind when He said, *"Blessed are those who mourn…"* It tells us, for instance, that loss affects all areas of life, throwing all areas out of balance, and that loss changes the meaning of life.

Loss Throws the Physical Area of Life Out of Balance

Following loss some people neglect their physical appearance and conditioning while others drive themselves relentlessly toward the goal of physical fitness. One individual declares, "I'm not hungry," and virtually stops eating while another eats everything in sight, either extreme signaling life is out of balance.

Loss Throws the Mental/Intellectual or Thinking Area of Life Out of Balance

Following loss, people experience difficulty processing thoughts, ideas, and experiences. Like the stereotypical absent-minded professor, in the wake of the loss of someone emotionally significant to us, we lose our train of thought in conversation, lock the car keys inside the car, and spend an inordinate amount of time looking for misplaced items or retracing our steps to restaurants and other public places to retrieve personal objects left behind.

It is characteristic of grieving individuals to drive to the market or commute to their place of employment with their minds "somewhere else." Consequently, while grieving individuals may—and often do—arrive at their destination unable to recall anything that happened during the trip.

Loss Throws the Inner or Spiritual/Psychological Area of Life Out of Balance

As this important area has both spiritual and psychological dimensions, imbalance may manifest itself as tears or as a questioning of the values that guide one's life.

Loss Throws the Social/Relational or People Area of Life Out of Balance

Loss tends to restructure personal relationships. Existing relationship networks shrink, opportunities for social interaction diminish somewhat, and the scope of social invitations received narrows significantly.

In many instances those who experience loss withdraw or lessen contacts with friends, relatives, and acquaintances. These people, in turn, often cut themselves off from or lessen contacts with those who have experienced loss.

Married couples, for instance, assume friends once married but now single would be uncomfortable or feel like fifth wheels at gatherings in which the majority of those present are coupled, prompting them to exclude those who have lost a spouse from parties and other social occasions.

In addition, in the wake of loss couples the least bit insecure in their marriages are likely to view friends who have lost a spouse, as threats.

Such thinking leads couples to perceive single friends as threats and exclude them from social gatherings. Individuals who experience loss by divorce can anticipate that a number of friends and acquaintances will sever or alter relationship with them. They can also expect to receive fewer invitations to gatherings in which both sexes are present, but that invitations to same-sex functions will increase.

Loss Throws the Financial/Economic Area Out of Balance

The trend in most instances is for family income to shrink following loss. Income shrinks significantly for females when marriages end in divorce because on the whole women earn less than men, and though alimony and/or child support funds are matters covered in decrees of separation and divorce, a significant portion of these funds are not paid.

◆   ◆   ◆

First, Psychology tells us loss throws all areas of life out of balance. It also declares loss changes the meaning of life.

In view of these findings, how are we to understand this universal experience that upsets the balance of life so completely? What is loss and in what way(s) is the meaning of life changed when loss occurs?

Bertha Simos defines loss as *"being deprived of or being without something one has had and valued...."*[1] I find it helpful to view loss as "anything that significantly changes the meaning of life."

Loss means our tie with someone emotionally significant to us has been severed and that person is no longer a present and active influence upon our life. When that someone is a Husband or Wife, the surviving spouse often feels he or she has changed, that they are not the same person now that they were prior to their loss.

To understand this altered sense of self, it is important to recall that in the process of living we develop and internalize patterns of thinking and acting—roles—which we use to express who we are to the world. Loss eliminates one or more of these roles and modifies others. Elimination or modification of any role important to us is perceived as a "change of self."

Loss Changes the Meaning of Life Significantly by Changing How We Feel about Ourselves

In the wake of certain losses (specifically desertion, separation, and divorce), self-esteem is affected. Those who experience the loss of a husband or wife report feeling less worthwhile than before because roles in which they felt good about themselves, and felt needed, have been eliminated or altered. In addition, surviving spouses are prone to feel the loss of a husband or wife has made them less desirable as these experiences are essentially the reverse of experiences leading to marriage.

Loss Changes Life Significantly by Eliminating Opportunities for Sharing Closeness

Augustine assessed the working of the human heart correctly when he observed, *"Our hearts are restless until they find their rest in Thee [God]."*

The heart being a symbol of the spirit, what Augustine said of the heart is also true of the spirit. In the same way the human heart is restless until it finds rest in God, so too, the human spirit is restless when its connection with someone emotionally significant is severed.

One person becomes significant to another in the deepest sense when what speaks loudest about them is their spirit. If beauty is what speaks loudest about a person and we connect on that basis, the relationship established can never be as meaningful as we want it to be because it is based on a quality which admittedly, is only skin deep and soon fades.

Connecting on any basis other than the spirit, relationships are likely to diminish in meaning and importance when that attribute fades. Only in the connecting of human spirits does the human heart find the rest it seeks.

◆   ◆   ◆

As marital relationships deteriorate sharing closeness tends to diminish. If reconciliation does not bring spouses together again, in time the distance between them becomes so great neither partner feels the bond of their union.

When marital partners no longer feel the bond of their union two things are certain. Their spirits have disconnected and their marriage has terminated "in fact." And while marriages that have terminated in fact are often retained in law, they are no longer complementary in nature as commitment to things necessary to sustain the oneness of relationship—*"mutual self-giving, mutual needs satisfaction, and mutual faith nurturing"*—is no longer mutually accepted and acted upon.[2]

At this point, partners in marriage are, in effect, two single adults living together, and their marriage, marriage "in name only" as partners whose spirits have disconnected no longer constitute a "one flesh union."

Little wonder among the difficult adjustments individuals must make following loss of a spouse is adjusting to the fact that they are no longer connected spirit-to-spirit to the person who has shared their life, and closely related, the necessity of overcoming fear of again connecting their spirit to that of another.

Unless fear of once again connecting spirit-to-spirit is overcome, future relationships are certain to lack the meaning people seek. People who fear connecting spirit-to-spirit are likely to establish emotional relationships before they are ready, or to establish relationships lacking substance, depth, and commitment. And should they elect to marry again before their fear of connecting spirit-to-spirit is overcome, the marriage is certain to lack the depth of intimacy desired as intimacy in marriage requires partners to be vulnerable to each other.

Loss Changes the Meaning of Life Significantly by Changing What it Means to Parent

Loss creates family units in which what it means to parent is changed. When loss comes through divorce, what it means to parent is changed for both Custodial and Non-Custodial parents.

Custodial parents discover parenting means assuming and exercising primary—and largely, unshared—responsibility for one or more children.

Non-Custodial parents discover parenting has changed as they are no longer involved directly in the parenting of their children on a daily basis, and time with their children is limited, especially in instances where they are involved in maintaining a second household.

◆   ◆   ◆

Understanding what loss is, and having identified ways loss significantly changes the meaning of life, "What is an appropriate response to loss?"

The most appropriate, and healthy response one can make to loss is grieve, as grieving performs functions that facilitate adjustment, restore balance to all areas of life, and bring comfort to those whose tie to emotionally significant persons has been severed.

Grieving helps those who experience loss adjust to the reality that the meaning of life has changed for them. It also helps them realize the futility of continuing to invest emotional energies in relationships no longer intact, and it provides time needed to incorporate the meaning of loss into the overall context of life.

The goal of grieving being adjustment, those who have lost someone emotionally significant to them must allow ample time for arriving at a level of emotional adjustment at which one approaches problems in a rational manner and copes effectively with the situations and circumstances encountered each day. Those who have experienced loss need time to restore order to their lives, develop the capacity of relating to other people effectively, and construct an optimistic outlook on life itself.

If, for any reason, the grieving process is short-circuited or sabotaged, people take unfinished business and emotional baggage into future relationships.

◆   ◆   ◆

The Second Beatitude can also be interpreted as saying, *"Oh the blessedness of those who are desperately sorry for the sorrow and the suffering of this world."*[3]

Essentially, Scripture presents four views of suffering. There is suffering understood as punishment for sin. Suffering viewed as a test of faith. Suffering understood as a corporate experience. And suffering perceived as a redemptive act.

In the Old Testament the predominant view of suffering is one that regards suffering as punishment for sin. *"It was conventional Hebrew belief,"* writes Mould, *"that prosperity and adversity were rewards and punishments direct from God. The righteous prospered because of his righteousness and and the wicked suffered for his sin."*[4]

It was this belief that prompted the disciples to question Jesus regarding the blindness of the man encountered in the temple at Jerusalem in John Chapter Nine.

That a man should have been born blind said to the disciples, "Someone has sinned! But who?" As the man in question had been blind since birth and could not have sinned to cause his own blindness, the disciples question whether he was born blind because of the sins of his parents.

While sin often results in suffering, it does not follow that all suffering is the result of sin. Bad things happen to good people.

Within the Body of Christ, however, there are some for whom the idea that bad things happen to good people simply doesn't fit within their theological framework. Therefore, when a good person suffers, individuals holding this position are apt to initiate a probe for sin in the life of the sufferer as Job's friends did.

To probe for sin in the life of people who are suffering is not in the spirit of the Second Beatitude. It forfeits the comfort promised in the Beatitude and does nothing to help people find meaning in their experience. It is, in fact, a remarkably insensitive thing to do as what people need when emotional ties are severed is to be blessed by the presence of someone whose purpose is to comfort.

If sin is responsible for suffering, as in many instances it is, of course, that is an issue between the sufferer and God. The issue for disciples and citizens of the Kingdom is whether they are willing to comfort those who are mourning.

While it is human to question why bad things happen to people regarded as good, the fact that people suffer at all raises the question of the role of God in human affairs. Though altogether simplistic, let it be said God is present and involved in human affairs purposefully and permissively.

God Acts Purposefully

Creation is meant to have meaning and purpose. It was Viktor Frankl who said meaning and purpose are the "whys" of life. For life to be abundant, it must have a why.

To give humankind a why, God acts purposefully. His acts are a perfect blending of what is best, what is right, and what is good.

God Acts Permissively

Though present and actively involved in the affairs of humankind, God also permits things to happen that are not in keeping with His Intent and Purpose, things that prompt humankind to ask, "Why?"

God acts in this manner because He has endowed humankind with a volitional center, or "will," to be used in making choices. The will with which men and women are created is free, free not only to make choices, but free to make choices not in keeping with God's intention, the ultimate choice being to reject God Himself.

Having endowed humankind with a will that is free, God does not override that will, for God, as Abraham Lincoln saw clearly, cannot be for and against the same thing at the same time. To override human will God would be going against Himself, in the process reducing humankind to the status of automaton. Rather than pursue such a course, God permits us to make choices that are neither in our best interest nor in keeping with His Purpose.

The flip side of the freedom to make choices, of course, is responsibility. We are responsible for the choices we make. Therefore, when in the exercise of our will we make choices not in keeping with God's Intention, and these choices bring suffering, God may or may not intervene.

Having freedom of choice means much of the suffering that elicits a "Why, God?" response from us is suffering we bring upon ourselves, suffering for which we, and not God, are responsible.

Therefore, rather than continuing to ask, "Why does God allow suffering?" which is to suggest God's way of doing things is either unfair or could be improved upon, might it not be wise to ask why rational beings use the freedom that is theirs in ways time, experience, and history have demonstrated bring suffering to themselves, their families, and the world at large?

Suffering as a Test of One's Faith

In the Book of Job, suffering is permitted as a test of faith. In conversation with God one day, Satan openly questions Job's motives for serving God, alleging Job serves God to get something. To Satan, Job's piety is essentially a bargain, a sort of divine/human *quid pro quo*, by which Job exchanges piety for privilege, In a nutshell, Satan suggests, "Job has found it pays to be religious."

So, God permits Satan to test Job by visiting calamity upon a man described "good and upright." God's instructions to Satan are simply, *"...everything he has is in your hands, but on the man himself do not lay a finger."* (Job 1:12 NIV)

First, Job's oxen and asses are carried away by the Sabaens and the servants keeping watch over them are slain. Next, fire falls from Heaven killing Job's sheep and their shepherds. Following that, Chaldean raiders steal his camels and slay their drivers. Finally, Job's sons and daughters perish in a hurricane. *"In all this,"* [calamity, disaster, and suffering] Scripture records, *Job sinned not, nor charged God foolishly."*

Yes, bad things happen to good people. Yet, in the stance they take toward what happens to them, good people transcend suffering, transforming it into something heroic, exemplary, and instructive.

Perhaps the factor that elevated the experience of Viktor Frankl in German prison camps to the level of the heroic and exemplary was his realization that everything can be taken from humankind except "the last of the human freedoms," which he identified as the freedom to choose what our response is toward the circumstances of our lives, especially ones that cannot be changed.

Is there not something exemplary, instructive, and heroic in the stance people take toward negative situations, circumstances, and predicaments, especially when, like Job, they neither sin nor charge God foolishly?

Suffering Is A Corporate Experience

This is the view of Deuteronomy 5:9, which regards humankind as a corporate body whose lineage can be traced to a common ancestor, Adam.

Oliver Wendell Holmes once said, *"Life is like a bus on which one's ancestors ride."* The essential truth in Holmes' remark is that humankind is interconnected. Words spoken from the Cross reflect Jesus' consciousness of the interconnectedness of humankind. In the sixth hour of His suffering Jesus cries out, *"Father, forgive them for they know not what they do."* (Luke 23:34) Paraphrased, what Jesus said was, *"Father, forgive them,* [for they don't understand that in hurting me they hurt themselves and others]. *"*

Suffering Is Redemptive

The prophets did not question why God permitted men to suffer because to them, God was God and that was that. Therefore, they were not troubled when Jehovah said, *"My thoughts are not your thoughts. Neither are your ways My ways…As the heavens are higher than the earth, So are my ways higher than your ways, And My thoughts than your thoughts."* (Isaiah 55:8-9)

Jesus intended His suffering to be redemptive. As the only begotten Son whom the Father gave to the world He loved, Jesus knew His death would be redemptive for all who believed. All who accepted His Death as redemptive would have eternal life. None would perish.

◆   ◆   ◆

While those who endure life's most distressing, disintegrating, and discouraging experiences, and those who care intensely for the suffering, sorrows, and needs of others will be comforted, the fundamental message of the Second Beatitude is, *"Blessed is the man whose heart is broken for the world's suffering and for his own sin...for out of his sorrow he will find the joy of God."*[5]

Luke's Gospel contains examples of two men desperately sorry for their sins. The first is Zacchaeus, a publican. The second, one of the criminals condemned to death along with Jesus.

In the period immediately following Peter's confession of Jesus as the Christ, Jesus began to show His disciples *"...that he must go to Jerusalem and suffer many things at the hands of the elders, chief priests, and teachers of the law, and that he must be killed and on the third day be raised to life."* (Matthew 16:21).

Evidently, Jesus and the disciples arrived in Jericho at an hour when travelers normally began looking for a place to spend the night. Zacchaeus, chief tax collector of the city, had heard of Jesus (quite possibly from the disciples Jesus had appointed to go ahead of Himself in (Luke 10:10-24), and wanted to catch a glimpse of him. However, being rather short (and from what we know of relationships between publicans and other Jews, we can assume Zacchaeus was not well liked), it was necessary for him to climb a sycamore tree.

Passing through the city Jesus noticed Zacchaeus in the tree and exercising the right accorded travelers to seek lodging, called out to him, *"Zacchaeus, come down immediately. I must stay at your house today."*

The hope of thoughtful hosts was that guests would find their hospitality so congenial that they would view the home of their hosts as their own. Consequently, guests were accorded great respect, every effort was made to meet their needs, and hosts did not speak of ownership.

We can only assume the hospitality accorded Jesus in the home of Zacchaeus left nothing to be desired. What we know for certain is that in the course of sharing his home with Jesus and the disciples, something happened that caused Zacchaeus to become sorrowful for his sins leading him to declare his intention to make restitution to those he had wronged.

As a first step, Zacchaeus proposed to give half his goods to the poor. The poor in this account are the *ptochoi*, which means the people to whom Zacchaeus was making restitution were the poorest of the poor, people on the bottom rung of the socioeconomic ladder, people living in abject poverty, people so helpless and destitute as to be reduced to begging as a means of survival.

The second step in Zacchaeus' plan of restitution called for restoring fourfold to any person falsely accused. As the ptochoi lacked standing or influence in the community and had no way of defending themselves, it seems reasonable to suppose Zacchaeus had falsely accused a number of them in the exercise of his office. His willingness to restore fourfold to anyone he had wronged was Zacchaeus' way of demonstrating contrition.

Recognizing Zacchaeus genuinely sorrowful for his sins, Jesus pronounces a blessing upon his house. *"Today is salvation come to this house."*

A second man depicted as desperately sorry for his sins is one of the malefactors sentenced to be crucified with Jesus. Though Scripture does not name these men, tradition has given one the name Dismiss.

On that first Good Friday three groups taunt Jesus, each calling upon Him to save himself if, indeed, He is who He says He is. The first to deride Him are the rulers or leaders of the Jews. The word used to identify these men—*arkontes*—suggests they were members of the Sanhedrin, the council of Jewish leaders who exercised civil jurisdiction over Jewish communities wherever they existed.(Luke 23:35)

Next to mock Jesus are the soldiers. Their words are, *"If you are the king of the Jews, save yourself."* (Luke 23:37) *He saved others, let him save himself if he is the Christ of God, the Chosen One."*

Last to mock Jesus is one of the men sentenced to be crucified. *"Aren't you the Christ?"* he asks. *"Save yourself and us."* (Luke 23:39)

Hearing Jesus addressed disrespectfully, Dismiss confronts the taunter. *"Don't you fear God,"* he asks, *"since you are under the same sentence? We are punished justly, for we are getting what our deeds deserve.*

But this man has done nothing wrong." Having reproved the man, Dismiss addresses Jesus, *"Jesus, remember me when you come into Your kingdom."* Jesus' words to Dismiss are words of comfort and hope. *"I tell you the truth, today you will be with me in paradise."*

While those who endure life's difficult, disintegrating, discouraging experiences and those desperately sorry for the sorrow and the suffering of this world will be blessed, the overarching declaration of the Second Beatitude is, "All who 'mourn' will be comforted."

In the time of Christ, mourning was a highly structured experience, much more so than is the case today. Customs permitted and encouraged active expressions of grief. Included among these were:

- Weeping and wailing

- Wringing of hands and outbursts of emotion

- Shaving part of one's beard and shaving one's head

- Throwing dust upon one's head

- Tearing or rending one's clothes, and

- Wearing sackcloth.[6]

Jacob's mourning for Joseph demonstrates the personal and public aspects of mourning. After selling Joseph to some Midianite merchants, his brothers sought to convince their father he was dead by sprinkling the blood of a goat on Joseph's coat of many colors and bringing it to Jacob. Supposing Joseph dead, Jacob rent his clothes, put on garments of sackcloth, and mourned for many days. (Genesis 37:23-34)

Families were actively involved in mourning. At the moment of death, members of the family initiated the ritual of mourning by emitting a loud wail recognized by all who heard it as signaling the occurrence of death, whereupon, neighbors proceeded to the house visited by death for the purpose of consoling and aiding the family.

While mourning, family members fasted, refrained from washing, and did not perfume their bodies.

It was customary for families to prepare the body for burial. After the body had been washed and robed, women in mourning anointed it with spices and ointments. It was this task left unfinished by the rapid approach of the Sabbath that would bring Mary Magdalene, Mary the mother of James, and Salome to the sepulcher early Easter morning.

As the climate of the Middle East is harsh and bodies were neither cremated nor embalmed, burial usually took place within twenty-four hours.

Religious services were not a part of the burial ritual in the ancient world. The body of the deceased was simply carried to the grave site on a bier, the poor buried in an open grave with stones piled upon it to protect the body from predators while members of middle and upper class families were buried in caves or tombs.[7]

Jesus was buried in the tomb of Joseph of Arimathea, whom Matthew describes as a rich man. (Matthew 27:57) In all likelihood, Joseph had intended the tomb as the burial place for members of his family. Using the tomb as the burial place of Christ meant Joseph's family could not be buried there as the rabbis forbade burial of one's fathers in the tomb where an executed man was laid.

Notes For Shepherds

The Second Beatitude has relevance for all who are called to the vocation of shepherd.

One of the principal benefits of interpreting this Beatitude literally is it teaches the value of welcoming each day *as* "the day that the Lord hath made."

All well and good as far as Mountaintop Days are concerned. Most of us find it easy to rejoice and be glad when our days are filled with optimism, enthusiasm, and success. Like the long, warm, lazy days of Summer, Mountaintop Days exhilarate and energize the human spirit.

We feel alive. In harmony with the universe. In tune with life. Life is good on the Mountaintop.

Though lacking the drive and pace, enthusiasm and excitement of Mountain Top Days, there is also ample reason for rejoicing in the Ordinary Days of life.

On the surface, Ordinary Days resemble the chilly, bleak, gray days of late November and early December when trees are bare and the land lies fallow. While at ground level nothing appears to be happening, beneath the surface the earth is preparing for a new season of productivity.

In the same way permitting land to lie fallow prepares it for an upcoming season of planting and harvest, Ordinary Days provide opportunities for our minds to lie fallow and our feelings to return to a state of quiescence.

Ordinary Days are times for shifting gears and stepping back, thus lessening the possibility that the pace and demands of life will stretch us beyond our limits and render us vulnerable to burnout.

Shepherds would be well-advised to learn the lessons of Ordinary Days and teach them to members of their flocks. As extended periods of stress and/or hyperactivity take a toll upon mind, body, and spirit, it seems wise to step back from time to time in order that one's mind might rest and one's emotions return to a quiet state. A wise and prudent use of life's Ordinary Days equips everyone for tasks certain to tax the mind and deplete one's physical and emotional reserves.

On their part, laymen would do well to remember the one who shepherds them is the only member of the human flock who has no shepherd, that his (or her) needs are similar to their own, and that failing to "shepherd the shepherd" puts that person at risk of being stretched beyond the limits of adaptability by the demands and stresses of their calling.

There is also reason to rejoice and be glad in the Valley Days of life. Valley Days are best likened to the harsh, cold days of Winter that limit the range of outdoor activities enjoyed during other seasons of the year. Yet, Valley Days serve purposes equally as important, though different, from those of either Mountaintop or Ordinary Days.

Essentially, Valley Days are times of testing and refining of human character. Thrust into the Valley by experiences that call into question who we are and what we hold to be important, it is in the Valley that we ask, "What kind of a person do I want to be? What is really important to me? What do I consider to be of lasting value?"

As important as these things are, perhaps, the most significant thing that happens in the Valley is we are introduced to Hope, the second of Paul's triumvirate of enduring values presented in First Corinthians, Chapter Thirteen.

Hope is the "Value of the Valley" precisely because it is future oriented. Hope is the faith that enables us to forget the things that lie behind (the experiences, the situations, and the circumstances that precipitated our walk through the Valley of Dark Shadows). It is hope that encourages us to press on toward the prize of the high calling of the abundant life.

The term for hope occurring most often in the Old Testament is one whose root meaning is very close to that of the Hebrew word for "believe." It implies rest, leaning on, trust, and confidence.[8]

Hope gives us the confidence to rest in the Lord and affirm there is a future, though the shape and dimensions of that future are indefinite.

It is Hope that energizes faith enabling us to move forward, confident that things are working for good in spite of present circumstances.

It is Hope that whispers, "Rejoice in this day. It was made for you. Be glad in it. It has much to teach you. When you shall have emerged from the dark shadows of the Valley you will see clearly that rejoicing and being glad even when life is uncertain, especially, when faced with circumstances that you cannot change injects a ray of Hope into each day."

From Hope we derive courage needed to walk through storms of sorrow and suffering, chin up high, unafraid of the shadows cast by experiences of loss.

Detriech Bonhoeffer personified hope as clearly as anyone in the Twentieth Century.

In the years preceding World War II, Bonhoeffer lived and lectured at Union Seminary in New York. As clouds of war gathered over Europe in the late 1930's and events began conspiring to bring about a struggle of global proportions, Bonhoeffer made the fateful decision to return to his homeland. Once there, he discovered he could not remain silent where Adolph Hitler and Nazism were concerned. In time, his opposition to the Third Reich earned him a cell in the infamous Buchenwald Concentration Camp where he remained for two years.

As the war progressed, Allies landed on French soil. As the armies drew near Buchenwald, the Gestapo hung Bonhoeffer.

Hanging Bonhoeffer was a futile gesture, of course, indicating once again that humankind had failed to learn a lesson taught time and time again, namely, that one does not silence the message by killing the messenger.

At his death, Bonhoeffer left the world a priceless heritage in the form of a collection of letters written from prison to parents and friends. They bear the stamp of his confidence in God and the role hope played in his life.

This confidence is best expressed in a letter written to a friend serving in the German air force. To his friend, Eberhard Bethge, Bonhoeffer wrote unforgettable words of hope. *"Whatever weakness, self reproach and guilt we attribute to these events [the war] in the events themselves is God. If we survive all this [meaning the war] we shall be able to see quite clearly that all has turned out for the best...and so we have every reason to hope."9*

To Bonhoeffer, it made sense to hope. In his life as well as his writings, He affirmed hope as more than a word religious people bandy about when they want to make others feel good and they can't think of anything else to say. Above all, Bonhoeffer affirmed hope never retreats from the difficulties associated with experiences that require human presence in life's Valleys of Dark Shadows.

A second benefit of interpreting the Second Beatitude literally is that it teaches all who are desperately sorry for the sorrow and suffering of this world will be blessed. Interpreting the Beatitude in this manner suggests humankind is linked in ways we have yet to appreciate, that between the peoples of the world there is a connectedness, a oneness of experience in which all participate.

Scripture contains two relational principles that help us understand and appreciate this interconnectedness and the responsibilities it implies. Taken from Genesis, the first principle states quite simply, *"...it is not good for the man to be [or live] alone."* (2:18) It is not good to be disconnected from others.

To be relationally alone is to be (or feel that one is) cut off, detached, or separated from, out of union, fellowship, communication, or association with, unrelated to or unloved by one's neighbor(s).

To be or feel that one is relationally alone in any of the ways named is to lack the confidence that our connection to those around us remains intact. If as the Yiddish proverb says, *"It is not good to be alone even in Paradise,"* how much more so a society in which relational vacuums increase in number and scope with each technological advance making it increasingly difficult to connect in friendship and build community.

Connecting in a compassionate way brings comfort to individuals struggling with the feeling that they are cut off from each other. Compassion affirms sorrow, suffering, and difficulty has not severed the relational bond between neighbors. In a word, compassion helps avoid relational aloneness.

The second relational principle is drawn from Matthew's Gospel. It helps us understand and appreciate the interconnectedness of humankind and the responsibility we have toward each other when one of us mourns. Simply stated, the principle is, *"Thou shalt love."* (Matthew 22:34)

Christ's admonition in Matthew 22:39 was to love one's neighbor as oneself. If, as Scripture teaches, God forgives us our trespasses as we forgive those who trespass against us, it seems equally certain that we will be comforted when we mourn to the extent that we comfort our neighbor when he (or she) is visited by sorrow and suffering.

Shepherds whose goal is abundant life for sheep in their care would do well to become acquainted with the concept of loss and what loss means in the lives of people.

Shepherds can help human sheep understand loss, persuade them that grieving is normal, to be expected, even desired following loss.

Shepherds can convince human sheep in their care of the importance of grieving losses thoroughly and completely.

Shepherds can assure those who mourn that while loss comes to everyone and grieving is always personal, there are many eager to come alongside and comfort them in their mourning.

Finally, a literal interpretation of the Second Beatitude suggests to mourn is to "…care deeply, to know godly sorrow for one's sin." Those who mourn in this manner can take comfort in the fact that sorrow for one's sins leads to the greatest comfort of all, the salvation of God. *"For God so loved the world that He gave His only begotten Son, that whoever [mourns because they are sorrow for personal sins committed], will be comforted with eternal life."*

5

Oh the Blessedness of the Meek for They Shall Inherit the Earth

❖

The Beatitude of Confidence and Self-Mastery

Having declared the Kingdom of God the reward of the poor in spirit, and comfort the blessing of those who mourn, Jesus spoke a third Beatitude. *"Oh the blessedness of the meek, for they shall inherit the earth."*

To understand the mind of Jesus and the implications meekness has for shepherds and members of the human flock in the living of the abundant life, it is essential to be clear regarding (a) what meekness is, (b) who are the meek, and (c) what it means to "inherit the earth."

What Is Meekness?

To persons living in the ambitious, aggressive, outer-directed society of the Twenty-First Century, meekness calls to mind mousy, withdrawn, retiring Casper Milquetoast, the stereotype of weakness, spinelessness, inadequacy, and ineffectiveness. Casper represents the kind of person who

- Adopts a subservient posture toward others

- Gives away their personal power, and

- Acquiesces to the ideas and opinions of others rather than risk advancing their own.

Most of us are acquainted with at least one person like Casper, someone who rarely calls attention to himself, is usually found on the fringe of situations requiring decision making, who rarely dons the mantle of leadership because to lead is to risk disfavor when decisions are not received favorably.

Meekness in contemporary society differs markedly from meekness in the Old Testament in which it is strength, balance, and reverence in men who *"obediently accept God's guidance, who humbly [accept] whatever God sends…whose life is strengthened and beautified by the gifts which God can give only to such a man."* [1]

Moses is described in Numbers 12:3 as *"a very humble man, more humble than anyone else on the face of the earth."* In this Israelite raised in Pharaoh's court meekness is reverence and humility manifested as strength and patience.

Subsequent to the establishment of the Hebrews in the Land of Promise, men of reverence and humility were replaced in the leadership structure of Israel by rich, prideful men who would move the nation in the direction of autocracy, despotism, and violence. [2]

No person is more closely identified with this movement or exerted greater influence upon the quality and direction of life in Israel than Solomon, son of David.

Raised in the shadow of an increasingly autocratic and violent father, Solomon had no qualms about eliminating rivals to the throne, putting to death anyone suspected of disloyalty, or wreaking vengeance upon whom his father's disfavor had fallen.

Accordingly, upon ascending to the throne, Abiathar, the priest, is banished to Anathoth because he had supported Adonijah's bid to seize the throne. Joab, commander-in-chief of the armies of Israel under

David is murdered within the Tent of Yahweh, and Shemei is executed for disobeying Solomon's command never to leave Jerusalem.

A corresponding shift in the understanding of meekness accompanied these significant changes in leadership and national direction. Meekness understood as reverence and humility in men like Moses evolved into meekness perceived as strength of character in men described as humble, poor, and lowly.

Jesus identified closely with such men. To those who labored to do the works of the law and those heavily laden by the demands of the Scribes, He said, *"Come unto me…take my yoke upon you and learn from me; for I am gentle [meek] and humble [lowly in heart]."* (Matthew 11:28-29)

Paul the Apostle exhorted Christians in Galatia to cultivate lowliness, meekness, long-suffering, and forbearance as these qualities promoted peace and helped maintain unity in the Spirit. (Ephesians 4:2) He listed meekness among the fruits of the Spirit in Galatians 5:23 as one of the things against which there was no law.

Aristotle also spoke of meekness. In the system of thought that bears his name, he posited meekness as the happy medium between extremes of being angry without cause and not being angry at all.

Who Are the Meek?

Thus far four perspectives of meekness have been introduced: meekness perceived as weakness, inadequacy, and ineffectiveness; meekness understood as reverence and humility, strength and patience; meekness perceived as character in men described as humble, poor, and lowly; and meekness as a happy medium between getting angry without cause and not getting angry at all.

In these views, the meek are confident, balanced individuals in whom dwell grace, virtue, and goodness manifested in reverence, humility, strength, patience, lowliness, and self-mastery.

Given the exemplary character of the meek and the inheritance promised them, the fact that Scripture does not provide specific instructions for acquiring meekness poses something of a problem.

However, it would appear that those who aspire to acquire the character of meekness must

- Bring their spirit under control

- Forgive those who trespass against them

- Accept anger as a part of the human makeup, and

- Control and express anger appropriately.

Meekness Requires Bringing the Human Spirit Under Control

The Greek word for meekness *(praus)* is used to describe a horse that can be ridden (or a dog that can be used to work sheep) because its spirit is under control.[3]

We use the term "breaking a horse," when speaking of the procedure by which the spirit of a horse is brought under control. The procedure, of course, is not intended to break the spirit of the horse, but rather to discipline it to respond to the commands of a rider.

The spirit of a dog is brought under control by training it to understand, accept, and respond to the commands of a handler. To be effective in the care and management of sheep, the shepherd must be able to issue commands to his dog confident of an immediate response.

Bringing the human spirit under control is a conscious decision on the part of men and women whose goal is to acquire the strength of character that merits the earth as an inheritance, whereas, bringing the spirit of a horse or dog under control is a decision made by the owner or someone interested in using the animal in some endeavor.

Meekness Requires Anger Be Under Control and Expressed in Ways That Do Not Lead to Sinning

To cultivate the strength of character called meekness requires accepting anger as part of our human makeup and learning to control and express it appropriately.

Neither Aristotle nor the Apostle Paul rule out anger as a legitimate part of the human makeup. Each seeks a middle ground, Aristotle between the extremes of getting angry without reason and not getting angry at all, Paul between being angry and allowing anger to lead one to sin.

Where anger is concerned, there are two issues. The first is to determine when anger is appropriate. The second is to express anger without sinning.

Generally speaking, psychologists and theologians consider anger appropriate when directed against injustice or the eradication of evil, but inappropriate when expressed as bitterness, hatred, revenge, and judgment, or when it results in abuse of any kind (emotional, physical, or spiritual), or incites people to sin (such as killing physicians who perform abortions). [4]

Anger in the New Testament is either a strong emotion or an expression of moral indignation. Jesus displayed both in an incident the Synoptic writers call, "The Cleansing of the Temple." (Matthew 21:12; Luke 19:45; John 2:14-15)

Anger as strong emotion motivated Jesus to fashion cords discarded by cattle drovers into a whip and drive from the Court of the Gentiles men defrauding worshipers in the sale of doves (required for making sacrifices) and in the exchange of foreign coins into shekels (the only form of exchange accepted as payment of the Temple tax).

Anger as moral indignation is what led Jesus to drive from the Temple men whose attitudes and activities had turned His Father's House (intended as a place of prayer), into a *"house of merchandise,"* (John

2:16), and a *"den of thieves"* (Matthew 21:13; Mark 11:15; Luke 19:46).

◆   ◆   ◆

Jesus expressed anger on other occasions as well, specifically when accused of violating Sabbath law.

Sabbath observance was an important element of Jewish life. Deuteronomy enjoined observance of the Sabbath (5:13-15). Following the example of God who rested from His labors upon completing the work of Creation, earliest observance of the Sabbath was as a day of rest. (Genesis 2:3) By the time of the Exodus, in addition to being a day of rest, the Sabbath had become a day on which no work was done.

Jesus' stance on Sabbath observance was a blend of religious and humanitarian reasoning, whereas, the Scribes and Pharisees approached the Sabbath from a perspective that placed ritual observance before showing mercy or meeting human need. The Scribes bolstered their position by hedging the Sabbath about with so many rules as to what was and was not lawful to do (there were, for instance, at least thirty-nine things that could not be done on the Sabbath) that the humanitarian and religious reasons for which the Sabbath was instituted were all but done away with.

In some, but not every instance, meeting human need or performing an act of mercy on the Sabbath was all that was needed to accuse someone of violating Sabbath law. In some instances, accusations of violating Sabbath law grew out of some aspect of an act of mercy. With regard to the healing of the paralytic at the Pool of Bethesda, it was Jesus' directive, *"Take up thy bed and walk"* that prompted the charge.

When used as a mode of transport, the mat on which the paralytic lay was considered a conveyance. Once he had been healed, however, the mat became a burden to be carried. Carrying a burden on the Sabbath was considered work. Working on the Sabbath was unlawful. As Jesus had instructed the man to take up his bed and walk, He was responsible for work being done, hence, the accusation of violating Sabbath law.

It annoyed Jesus that the Pharisees placed ritual observance above showing mercy or meeting human need.

It disturbed Him that the hardness of their hearts prevented religious leaders of Israel from rejoicing in the performance of acts of mercy simply because they were performed on the Sabbath Day.

It exasperated Him that men prominent in the religious life of Israel would seize upon acts of mercy (such as the healing of a paralytic, the healing of a man with a withered hand, and the healing of a man born blind) to accuse Him of violating the spirit and intent of Sabbath law.

It distressed Him that the men who stood at the heart of religious life in Israel were blind to the fact that He was Messiah.

Suggestions for Controlling One's Anger and Expressing it Appropriately

Though fully God, in the flesh Jesus was also fully human. Anger was as much a part of His makeup and experience as our own.

Anger is a necessary and useful part of our makeup. Our task is to learn to control our anger and express it in ways that enable us to "be angry, but sin not."

Consider the following guidelines for controlling and expressing anger appropriately.

Decide What is Important and Emphasize It

When we are clear as to what is important to us, it lessens the possibility of becoming angry over matters trivial and inconsequential. For example, saying grace before meals is important to many people. If this is the case for you, emphasize the saying of grace that others will know you feel strongly about it.

Decide What Is Unimportant and Forget It

Nothing is gained by becoming angry over things trivial or non-essential. Some things are just not worth getting worked up about. Decide what is unimportant and forget it.

Acknowledge Your Anger

As we go about our routines each day, we have hundreds of interactions. While most are happy, positive, and constructive, some are not. A reckless motorist endangers life on the freeway by changing lanes improperly or riding our bumper in heavy traffic. A colleague gets the promotion for which we are clearly the best qualified and most logical candidate. Opportunities for making the kind of contribution we want to make and are capable of making go to others because they have the ear of the power brokers or those charged with the responsibility of programming events.

It has been said, "What happens to us in life isn't nearly as important as how we feel about what happens to us." None of the examples given are life-and-death matters in and of themselves, yet they easily take on life-and-death seriousness when our feelings are aroused.

We know, for example, that talents and abilities become dull and sometimes are lost when not used. Therefore, when our goals are thwarted, our talents and abilities ignored, or we feel discounted in areas important to us, what we feel is anger which can, and sometimes does, lead us to sin.

Clearly, in warning Christians to, *"Be angry, but sin not,"* Paul was not implying anger itself is sinful. He was saying, *"express your anger in ways that are safe, healthy, and responsible."*

In many instances, simply being aware of anger is sufficient to control it as awareness leads to acknowledgment, acknowledgment to acceptance, and acceptance to the initiation of strategies and mechanisms of control.

Acknowledging one's anger can be accomplished by means of an inner dialogue that goes something like this, "This anger is mine. I'm aware of it. I own it. It is a part of me at the moment. Only I can do something about it."

To find and remain in the middle ground Paul said lies between anger on the one hand and sinning on the other requires understanding the process by which one moves from being angry to sinning.

In general, our thoughts are in harmony with our system of values. Feelings, in turn, follow our thoughts, and behaviors follow our feelings.

To remain in the middle ground and express anger without permitting anger to lead us to sin is a matter of imposing one's will at some point before behavior leads us to sin.

There is virtue when angry in adhering to the practice of counting to "10" before acting. Counting functions as a measure of control because in the time required to count from one to ten, the person who is angry has opportunity to (a) reflect upon what he (or she) is feeling, (b) determine whether their anger is appropriate or inappropriate, (c) decide what they are going to do with their anger, (d) ponder the possible consequences of expressing anger, and (e) reflecting upon whether they are willing to live with the consequences of expressing anger.

Confess Anger to God and Others

The stumbling block with respect to controlling human anger is the ability to perceive things correctly. God's anger is appropriate because His perceptions are accurate, while human anger is often inappropriate because human perception is faulty. If the lens of perception were cleansed as Robert Blake suggests, we would see things as they are and anger would be less a problem.

Seeing things as they are enables us to understand some situations simply do not warrant anger.

Meanwhile, confessing one's anger to God and others helps retain it within limits that are not only safe and acceptable, but short of sinning.

Confessing anger lessens the likelihood that we will dwell on situations, circumstances, or entertain thoughts that arouse anger. It has been said in ways too numerous to recall that what we think about expands and grows stronger whether the focus of our thinking is success or failure, health or sickness, forgiving those who trespass against us, or getting even.

Anger dwelt upon at length is likely to get out of hand. When anger breaks the bonds of self-control, we tend to blow up or clam up. Either way, anger can be, and often is, inappropriate and destructive to relationships. *"When one blows up,"* writes Jay Adams, *"his emotional energies are aimed and fired at someone else. When he clams up, bodily tensions are released within oneself. In both cases, the emotional energies of anger are wasted. In both they are used 'destructively.' In neither instance are they used constructively to solve problems."*[5]

Meekness Requires Forgiving Those Who Trespass Against Us

Forgiveness is a fascinating, yet, complex subject, one that has receded into the background as a pattern of response to offense and trespass in a society that, while not outwardly opposed to the giving and receiving of forgiveness, does little beyond giving lip service to the idea of forgiveness as a pattern of response.

Regrettably, ours is a society in which violence is accepted as a way of life, therefore, getting even is often the method of response selected for resolving differences. In contemporary society, to speak of forgiving those who trespass against us is to risk being labeled a wimp or loser rather than applauded, appreciated, and admired for possessing strength of character sufficient to rise above acts of trespass, hurt, and offense.

As a consequence of these shifts in consciousness, we are not at all sure what forgiveness is and what it requires of us. Uncertain as to what forgiveness is, it is extremely difficult to distinguish behaviors for which "I'm sorry" is appropriate from ones for which forgiveness is the only remedy.

In addition, society and its people have become so adept at rationalizing trespasses and offenses that the practice has become an art form. We speak of making mistakes, rather than admit to wrongdoing. We allude to misdeeds as errors of judgment (which, in many instances they are, of course) rather than say, "I have wronged you. I'm sorry. Please forgive me."

In the fourth place, we are almost completely in the dark as to why we forgive those who trespass against us.

Scripture Identifies Debts, Trespasses, Transgressions and Sins As Offenses Requiring Forgiveness

The Greek word translated debts or trespasses in the Lord's Prayer *(opheilama)* is derived from a noun meaning to owe. Matthew uses this word when speaking of offenses serious enough as to require reparation on the part of an offender. (Matthew 6:12)

The same word is used in Romans 15:27 to denote debts for which payment is due. Debts and trespasses in the Lord's Prayer are the equivalent of transgressions in Matthew 6:14 and sins in Luke 11:43.8

Accordingly, when we petition God to forgive us our trespasses (or debts), what we are doing is acknowledging ourselves debtors to God and trespassers against Him. We pray for forgiveness because, whether labeled sins, debts, trespasses, or transgressions, our offenses are serious enough that they can neither be denied, excused, minimized, nor condoned. Neither can they be absolved by a socially correct, "I'm sorry." Forgiveness is the only remedy.

What Is Forgiveness?

Forgiveness is both act and process. It is either a response consciously chosen or a process intentionally set in motion in the wake of offense or trespass. In either case, forgiveness always involves an offender, an offended, and an offense.

Psalm 103 is the most explicit example of forgiveness in Scripture. In particular, it demonstrates what forgiveness is and what it is not. It dissects the anatomy of forgiveness and presents strong support for saying sound theology is healthy psychology.

David introduces the subject of forgiveness by noting first what God does not do, namely, He does not deal with us according to our sins nor requite or reward us according to our iniquities. (v. 12).

Though we commit offenses against God by acting in ways that thwart His Purpose and Intent, He does not deal with us as we deserve. Neither does He retaliate by returning offense for offense.

God's example teaches the wisdom of foregoing retaliation and getting even as patterns of response. To entertain thoughts of retaliation or getting even is as unwise as it is unhealthy as neither response serves a healthy, constructive purpose.

No one profits from a philosophy of life that demands an "eye for an eye and a tooth for a tooth." This century alone offers more than a few examples of how difficult it is to conclude and maintain a just and lasting peace between nations whose relations are governed by the retaliatory principle, "An eye for an eye and a tooth for a tooth."

Time after time, especially, since the conclusion of World War II, the actions of nations have confirmed trading an eye for an eye and a tooth for a tooth accomplishes nothing beyond keeping the wheels of retaliation well-oiled and perpetuating the delusion that a climate of forgiveness is created by getting even with those who commit offenses against us.

Thankfully, in our more detached, objective moments, we recognize an eye-for-an-eye approach to life never results in satisfaction and inner peace because it is based on two assumptions, both false, the first being that it is possible to get even with those who commit offenses against us, and the second, that inner peace will be ours once we have done unto others as they have done unto us.

If then God does not deal with us according to our sins nor requite us according to our iniquities, what steps does He take in forgiving those who commit offenses against Him?

Removal: First Step In Forgiving

God's first step in forgiveness is to remove the sins of the offender. To where does God remove trespasses and offenses committed against Him, and once removed, what does He do with them? The Psalmist's answer to the first question is, *"So far as the East is from the West, so far has He removed our transgressions,"* while Isaiah's answer to the second is, *"God remembers them no more."* (Isaiah 43:25)

To appreciate the picture of forgiveness presented in Psalm 103, it is essential to view God's removal of human transgressions against a background of Old Testament thinking, in particular, (a) how the Hebrews determined direction and assigned meanings to the primary points of the compass, (b) how the location of Palestine on the land bridge connecting Asia and North Africa influenced the naming of the points of the compass, and (c) the tendency of writers of Hebrew poetry to refer to the cardinal points of the compass when their intent is to convey "totality" or communicate the idea of *"everywhere."*

The Hebrews determined direction by dividing the world into four parts or "corners," and assigning each corner, or direction, a name. The direction of primary interest was the East. In the Old Testament, terminology used when speaking of the East (and meanings attached to this reference point) is derived from language having to do with the sunrise *(mizrakh)* or from derivatives of the root meaning "before, in front of Him."[6]

Like peoples everywhere, the Hebrews oriented themselves by facing the place where the sun rose each morning. They spoke of this place as "the place of dawning." Facing the place of dawning meant the sun was literally "before" or "in front" of one's face.[7] In the same way, they thought of the West as the direction that lay behind one's face.

The North also held considerable interest for the Hebrews because of the location of Palestine on the geographical land bridge connecting Asia and North Africa. The history of this land bridge, which historians have labeled "the Fertile Crescent," is one of nomadic migration and struggle between nations bent on expansion and conquest.

The location of Palestine being what it is, when policies and interests of empires at either end of the Fertile Crescent called for expansion or conquest, likely as not, Palestine was in the line of march. As Palestine was more likely to be invaded from the upper rather than the lower end of this land bridge, the Hebrews called the direction of anticipated invasion "North" (derived from a Hebrew word meaning "look out"), and erected their first line of defense—the watch tower—facing that direction.[8]

The word for "South" comes from a Hebrew word meaning "dry country." By and large, when Scripture speaks of the South, the reference is to the Negev, an ill-defined geographical area extending southward some seventy miles from Hebron in the direction of North Africa. Throughout history, at least until modern times, the Negev has served as a buffer against an invasion from the South (because of a serious shortage of water and the necessity of crossing a series of mountains running East and West through the area). [9]

Comprehending the meaning which the cardinal points of the compass had for men of the Old Testament enriches greatly our understanding of forgiveness as act and process. In effect, by using the phrase *"as far as the East is from the West,"* David is saying, "God removes our sins totally and completely from 'in front of or before' his face (the East) to a place as far in the 'rear of His face' as is possible (the West)."

Not only does God remove our sins totally and completely, He does a second, and equally remarkable thing. *"He remembers them no more."* (Isaiah 43:25)

At first glance, it would appear Isaiah is saying God forgets our sins, and while the effect of removing sins and transgressions to a place that cannot be pinpointed is tantamount to forgetting them, the fact remains that God does not forget our sins nor does forgiveness require that we forget offenses committed against us.

Forgiveness neither involves nor requires offenses be forgotten as forgetting would forfeit the function of experience, which is to teach. It would forfeit, as well, the value of experience as a reservoir of direction, guidance, counsel, and instruction needed to live abundant lives.

So, having removed our transgressions, rather than forget them, what God does is remember them in a special way. "He remembers them—against us—no more."

That's what true forgiveness is, remembering offenses and trespasses against an offender no more! Forgiveness is doing unto those who trespass against us as God does when men sin against Him, removing the their sins against us to a place in our lives as far as the East is from the West in the universe, remembering them against an offender no more, and refusing to recall offenses to mind once they have been forgiven.

One of cruelest things humans do to each other is call to mind offenses that have been forgiven. Remembering offenses which an offender has reason to believe have been forgiven suggests in the mind of the offended party a debt remains to be paid, reparation is expected. Equally important, it characterizes the spirit of the offended party as vengeful, their theology, unsound, their psychology, unhealthy, and their relationships, uncertain.

Forgiveness understood as remembering offenses against an offender no more is admittedly a high and lofty standard, hard to reach and difficult to maintain, as humankind does seem to walk with feet of clay.

So, why does God forgive human trespasses? God's answer through Isaiah is, "for my own sake," (Isaiah 43:25) to which the Psalmist adds, because "He remembers we are dust." (Psalm 103:14) Likewise, when others trespass against us, we forgive them for our own sake, because psychologically forgiveness is healthy, theologically it is sound, and relationally, it is the best thing to do. We forgive those who commit offenses against us because

- Like us, they too, are dust

- We have no need to reap in body, mind, and soul the destructive harvest which negative, toxic, thoughts, feelings, and behaviors are sure to bring

- We are unwilling to continue contaminating ourselves by holding on to hurts, harboring grudges, and entertaining thoughts of retaliation, and

- It is not in our best interest to withhold forgiveness and thus permit an already difficult interpersonal situation to continue until it erupts in conflict.

- Finally, we forgive because in the unlikely event that we should succeed in exacting an eye for an eye or securing reparation for trespasses committed, we would still be empty, unfulfilled, and void of peace in the core of our being where we had expected to experience satisfaction.

Writing in *Psychology Today*, Beverly Flannigan makes a most uncommon observation. *"In a way,"* she says, *"forgiveness is only for the brave."*[10] To forgive, we must be brave enough to confront our pain, courageous enough to choose forgiveness over resentment and hatred, gallant enough to take the steps forgiveness requires, and heroic enough to refuse to retaliate or attempt to get even.

Above all else, we forgive out of obedience to God.

In the Lord's Prayer, we pray, *"Forgive us our trespasses (or debts) as we forgive those who trespass against us (or, are in debt to us)."* On the subject of forgiveness, Jesus said, *"If you forgive men when they sin against you, your heavenly Father will also forgive you. But if you do not forgive men their sins, your Father will not forgive your sins."* (Matthew 6:14-15)

◆   ◆   ◆

One task remains with regard to the Third Beatitude, and that is to ascertain what Christ meant when He said the meek would "inherit the earth."

Scholars are somewhat divided as to the meaning of this phrase because inheritance is used in both legal and theological contexts in Scripture.

Legal Context of 'Inherit The Earth'

Within Judaism, inheritance meant primarily, "inherit the land." Under Hebrew law, only blood relatives on the father's side were qualified to inherit. The order of succession spelled out in the Book of Numbers (27:8-11) entitled the firstborn son to inherit his father's land and a double portion of his father's possessions (that is, twice the portion allotted a brother), because as the firstborn he was expected to assume responsibility for family members when he succeeded his father as head of the family.

Theological Context of *'Inherit the Earth'*

In the Old Testament, the idea of inheritance reflects God's covenant relationship with His people. In general, to inherit meant coming into possession of something promised by God, the land of Canaan being a primary example.

As Israel moved progressively from wanderer to settler to nation to kingdom to divided kingdom to captivity, the covenant established at Sinai was augmented by a new, spiritual covenant written upon the hearts of men. (Jeremiah 31:31) With the initiation of this covenant, God's relationship with His people is understood in spiritual rather than physical terms.

Therefore, in the New Testament, to inherit the earth means to inherit the Kingdom of God.

Accordingly, the phrase in the Lord's Prayer closest to the heart of the meek is the one that affirms, *"Thy Kingdom come, thy Will be done on earth as it is in heaven,"* because it is their understanding that the Kingdom of God comes as men attain a level of personal development at which their lives are characterized by self-mastery and self-control.

With life in balance, the meek are able to be angry when anger is appropriate and express anger without sinning.

It has been said by those who misunderstand the true nature of meekness that the "meek will never inherit the earth because they are too shy to ask for it." But, the point of Scripture is that the meek need not ask. They need not because it is God's desire to bestow the Kingdom upon those who commit themselves to Him, whose lives are dedicated to His purpose in the world, those through whom His will flows.

Notes To Shepherds

If your aspiration is to be a shepherd of human sheep, set meekness as the goal of your life. Include on the agenda of each day the task of elevating the level of self-control and self-mastery you exercise over yourself.

As you are at the hub of hundreds of interactions each day, learn as much about yourself as you can possibly learn. Pursue self-knowledge. Read extensively in the fields of psychology, communication, poetry, and history, especially, biographical history.

Be aware of and alert to your physical/emotional signals that say, "There is something here for me, something personal and important from which I can benefit."

Whether positive or negative in nature, everything you read speaks to you in some way. If something seems to jump out at you, accept that as an indication that the text is speaking to you. If you recoil from something, accept that as a signal as well.

In either case, ask yourself, "What is the material saying to me at this point? About myself. About my relationship to God. What can I learn from what I'm reading that will enable me to give myself in a more potent manner to the care and management of human sheep in my care?"

Just as everything you read has the possibility of teaching you something about yourself, everyone you meet tells you something about your self, and by an extension of thought, your relationship with God.

Let's suppose you are on your way home. At the newsstand on the corner stands a man whose face is unwashed, whose clothes are tattered, whose hair is straggly.

What does that scene tell you about the man?

Actually all that scene is capable of telling you is a man with unwashed face, straggly hair, and tattered clothes is standing at the corner newsstand.

Let's suppose, however, that upon noticing the man you said to yourself, "He doesn't care how he is dressed. He probably hasn't had a bath in a month and for sure he doesn't own a hair brush."

In your response, you did two things. First of all, you identified with him. You put yourself in his place and said, "If I were standing at a newsstand in tattered clothes with straggly hair and unwashed face, I would wouldn't care how I was dressed. I probably would not own a hair brush, and, most likely, not have had a bath for a month."

Then you judged him. You said, "Because your clothes are tattered, your hair straggly, and your face unwashed, you must be a certain kind of person."

And you don't know. It is altogether possible that the man at the newsstand had just left his job and has not had time to shower, change his clothes, and brush his hair. All sorts of explanations are possible. Yet, the judgment you made is certain to influence how you relate to the person before you.

Acceptance is the strength of character that enables the meek to acknowledge "what is," without allowing how they feel about such things as a sloppy appearance to alter their commitment to meeting the needs and acting in the best interest of the people they meet each day.

Shepherds whose objective is meekness would do well to examine the creedal statements of service clubs for clues to greater self-mastery and self-control.

For example, the Creed of Optimist International says, *"Be So Strong That Nothing Can Disturb Your Peace of Mind."*[11]

To be so strong that nothing disturbs our peace of mind requires that we become inwardly confident and secure in who we are.

Inner confidence and security is influenced by two types of input—positive input in the form of a compliment or affirmation and negative input in the form of a criticism or put-down.

The interesting thing, however, is whether positive or negative, we allow input into our mind only when (a) we agree with it, or (b) we think we deserve it. If we think we deserve a compliment or we agree with it, we will allow it to enter. Allowing a compliment to enter, we become one compliment more confident and secure than before.

If we agree with a criticism or think we deserve a put-down, we will allow that to enter and disturb our peace of mind, rendering us one thought less confident and secure than before.

'Make Everyone Feel There Is Something in Them'

Generally speaking, people want to feel there is something in them, that they have whatever is needed to reach their goals. Yet, many are not at all certain they have what is needed to succeed.

People confident and secure in themselves are able see things in others that these people do not see in themselves. If courageous enough to tell them, and unselfish enough to commit themselves to personal growth in that person, things begin to happen.

'Look at the Sunny Side of Everything and Give Every Creature You Meet a Smile'

Smiles are outward manifestations of a confident and secure person, one who looks on the bright side of things, puts the best possible interpretation upon situations and circumstances, and thinks the best of people.

It is good to give everyone we meet a smile because smiles convey acceptance, and, in the same way soft answers turn away wrath, smiles shed light on the human path. There is more truth than generally recognized in the observation that "smiles are as catching as the measles and a lot more pleasant."

'Think Only the Best, Work Only for the Best, and Expect Only the Best'

Both psychology and theology encourage people to think, work, and expect only the best, and refuse to settle for less in themselves and others.

Being made in the image of God is what elevates humankind above all God's creatures. Thinking, working, and expecting only the best and refusing to settle for less in oneself and others, is using the resources of that image as God intended. As we discipline ourselves to think, work, and expect the best of ourselves and others we glorify the one in whose image we are created and we grow in self mastery and self control essential to meekness.

'Be Just as Enthusiastic About the Successes of Others as You Are About Your Own'

One of the more admirable human traits is the capacity to celebrate the success of others, to rejoice in the fact that something good has happened in the lives of others, who like ourselves, need to experience success.

The capacity to celebrate rather than resent or be filled with envy when good things happen to others is the sign of a gracious spirit.

It is well to rejoice that someone "did it," "got it," or "reached it," "it" being something important to them.

It is good to celebrate the good things that happen to others, to applaud even when what happens to others are desires and dreams that remain unfulfilled in our own lives. Cheering when good things happen to others is one of the noblest and most unselfish of all human responses. Reveling in the successes of others as if they were our own is a sure sign that we are moving toward greater self-mastery and self-control.

'Forget the Mistakes of the Past and Press On Toward Greater Achievements in the Future'

Life is a relentless, unswerving flow of experiences that shape and mold us. In a sense, life is like a string stretching from birth to death on which experiences are threaded in the way pearls are strung to make a necklace.

Whether positive or negative, constructive or destructive, whether thrust upon us or the product of unwise personal choices, each experience contributes to our being the person we are today. Forgetting the mistakes we've made and pressing toward greater achievements in the future is moving toward self-mastery and self-control using experience to best advantage.

'Give So Much Time to the Improvement of Yourself That You Have No Time to Criticize Others'

Each person has a mental image of themselves in their mind. Esteem for the image we have of ourselves is an assessment of our worth and value in our own eyes. While our personal worth and value is constant in the eyes of God, esteem for who we are in our own eyes tends to fluctuate, especially, when

- Disappointed or discouraged
- Our tie with some emotionally significant to us has been severed.
- Life seems to throw us curves and
- Things don't go well for us.

Likewise, it is hard to affirm ourselves as persons of worth and value when

- We feel discounted or put down and
- Individuals sin or trespass against us.

At such times we are prone to say or think, "If I were really important or worthwhile, these things would not be happening" and to employ negative strategies such as criticizing others in order to feel good about ourselves.

One thing is certain. Negative strategies never help us feel good. Tearing others down accomplishes nothing apart from broadcasting the fact that we are having difficulty esteeming ourselves. And criticizing others succeeds only in revealing our weaknesses and shortcomings, identifying our fears, and placing obstacles in the path of wholeness, completeness, mastery, and control.

When tempted to criticize others, it is a good idea to give more time to the improvement of ourselves.

'Become Too Large for Worry, Too Noble for Anger, Too Strong for Fear, and Too Happy to Permit the Presence of Trouble'

To be sure, becoming too large for worry, too noble for anger, too strong for fear, and too happy to permit the presence of trouble is a tall order, but it is better to aim high and miss than to aim low, and hit.

In the same way we applaud those who detach from the world and things of the world and place their trust in God, and appreciate those who come alongside their neighbor (when the evil and wickedness of the world results in suffering, sorrow, insult or injury), we hold in high regard individuals who aspire to a level of personal living at which men and women are too large for worry, too noble for anger, too strong for fear, and too happy to permit the presence of trouble.

And it is true that as we move toward self-mastery and self-control fewer things disturb our peace of mind. As we discipline ourselves to think only the best, work only for the best, and expect only the best of ourselves and others, and we are as enthusiastic about the successes of others as we are about our own, we move confidently toward the future and greater achievements. As we give so much time to the improvement of ourselves that we have no time to criticize others, we become too large for worry, too noble for anger, and too strong to permit the presence of trouble.

Finally, shepherds, rejoice and be glad in each day. It is generally accepted that attitude sets the tone for our days. When the tone set is one of rejoicing and being glad, each situation faced and circumstance experienced becomes an opportunity for injecting hope into the lives of those whose lives touch yours.

Individuals stuck in the throes of negative life situations and circumstance find sharing company with shepherds who rejoice and are glad each day the Lord gives helps change their perspective. Instead of seeing only gloom and doom, people begin seeing possibilities. Strive toward that strength of character, that balance characteristic of a finished product. Work diligently toward acquiring that level of self-mastery and self-control that places you among the meek in order that the world will be your inheritance.

6

Oh the Blessedness of Those Who Hunger and Thirst after Righteousness

❖

The Beatitude of Desire

The Fourth Beatitude is set against a background of concern for the basic necessities of life.

Poverty was widespread in the time of Jesus. The objection raised by Judas and the other disciples when expensive ointment is used to anoint Jesus reflects awareness of the plight of people and the conditions under which they lived. (John 12:1-8) To the Twelve, the ointment would have served a higher purpose had it been sold and the money used to relieve the distress of the poor. (Matthew 26:10-14)

◆　　　◆　　　◆

In First Century Palestine concern for the basic necessities of food, clothing, and shelter was an issue for many. While the working poor made just enough money to keep body and soul together, the desperately poor lived in abject poverty unable to meet their own needs. Clearly, these people would have benefited had the ointment used to anoint Jesus been sold and the money used on their behalf.

The poor were not without hope, however. Loans made to relieve their distress carried no interest. Permitted to glean fields that had been harvested, they also enjoyed the produce of the land during Sabbatical years and their debts were wiped from the books. In addition to these benefits, Jewish authorities collected and distributed alms to the poor and an offertory for them became part of the service of the synagogue.[1]

◆   ◆   ◆

The poor benefited greatly from the growth of the practice of alms giving. Giving alms was a religious act, a way of opening one's hand for the purpose of relieving the stress of the unfortunate.

With the passing of time, the people came to believe giving alms had redemptive, atoning benefits for those giving them. By the time Jesus began his public ministry, giving alms was equated with righteousness.

Regrettably, giving of alms had also become a way of calling attention to one's self.

Jesus spoke to the issue of the proper spirit in which men were to perform religious acts in words too direct to be misunderstood. *"Be careful,"* He said, *"not to do your acts of righteousness [practice your piety before men] to be seen by them."* (Matthew 6:1)

Using religious acts to call attention to oneself is "ostentation." Ostentation dilutes the genuineness of religious acts by shifting the focus from the One who is worshiped to the one who is worshiping.

Jesus condemned the Pharisees for using religious acts to call attention to themselves. Of them He said, *"Everything they do is done for men to see..."*

To be seen of men, the Pharisees enlarged the size of their phylacteries, lengthened the tassels on their outer garments, sought places of honor at feasts, clamored for the important seats in the synagogue, solicited salutations in the marketplace, and encouraged people to address them as rabbi.

◆   ◆   ◆

Phylacteries were leather pouches or cases containing portions of the Law worn by Jewish males (thirteen years of age or older) on the forehead, upper arm, and next to the heart during the recital of morning prayer on all days save Sabbath and festival days.[2] Intended as a reminder to keep the Law, phylacteries were called "places of preservation." However, in the time of Jesus they were regarded as amulets or charms capable of warding off evil and attracting good.[3]

The Pharisees also called attention to themselves by lengthening the tassels attached to the corners of an outer garment called a "himation." Made from a large rectangular piece of cloth, the himation protected the wearer against the elements and served as a covering at night.[4] It was the hem of this kind of garment worn by Jesus that the woman subject to bleeding sought to touch, believing that, if she could just touch the clothes of Jesus, she would be healed. (Mark 5:25-28)

In addition to enlarging their phylacteries and lengthening the tassels on their outer garments, the Pharisees also called attention to themselves by seeking places of honor at feasts and in the synagogue.

Feasts were occasions for celebration in the First Century. Whether entertaining friends or observing some special occasion, it was customary to send invitations by means of a servant and to follow up that invitation with a reminder on the day of the event. This is the procedure followed by the host in Luke's Parable of the Great Feast (14:15-24).

Guests were expected to dress appropriately. Honored guests wore gala white garments. To come to a feast wearing one's everyday clothes was an affront. Arriving at the site of the feast, guests could expect their host to greet them with a kiss, provide water for washing dust from their feet, and anoint their head with perfumed oil. Jesus faulted his host in Luke Seven because these courtesies had not been extended.

It was the prerogative of the host to determine seating arrangements. The "chief seats," or "places of honor" at feasts were nearest the host.

Jesus warned against taking these places unless invited to do so. *"When someone invites you...do not take the place of honor, for a person more distinguished than you [the designated guest of honor, perhaps] may have been invited. If so, the host who invited both of you will come and say to you, 'Give this man your seat.' Then, humiliated, you will have to take the least important place."* (Luke 14:7-9)

Places of honor in the synagogue were seats reserved for elders of the community. These stood facing the congregation in front of an elevated platform (called the bema) on which stood the desk from which Scripture was read. The Pharisees coveted these seats because the people who occupied them were esteemed important in the eyes of the community.

◆   ◆   ◆

Jesus specifically warned against ostentation when giving alms, offering prayers, and fasting. He likened calling attention to oneself when offering alms to sounding a trumpet. *"When you give to the needy,"* He said, *"do not announce it with trumpets as the hypocrites do in the synagogues and on the streets, to be honored by men [to be seen of them]."* (Matthew 6:2)

When the motive of alms givers was a genuine desire to relieve the distress of a neighbor, alms were offered with such grace that the left hand of the almsgiver did not know what the right hand was doing. When the purpose for giving alms was to call attention to oneself, almsgivers sought a place (such as a street corner) where they were certain to be seen and offered their alms in a manner that called attention to themselves.

◆   ◆   ◆

Jesus also warned against ostentation in prayer. *"When you pray,"* He said, *"do not be like the hypocrites, for they love to pray standing in the synagogues and on the street corners to be seen by men."* (Matthew 6:5a)

It was not that men stood while offering their prayers (as standing was the usual posture in which prayers were offered) or that prayers were offered in the synagogue or on the street corner. What concerned Jesus was the attitude in which men prayed and the purpose for which prayer was offered, because prayer, like the giving of alms, had become a means of calling attention to the one who prayed.

Prayer is, perhaps, the most personal of all acts of piety. John Powell speaks of prayer as a *"communication in a relationship of love, a speaking and a listening in truth and in trust."*[5]

The purpose of prayer is dialogue, a speaking and listening to God. When used to call attention to one's self, prayer ceases to be dialogue, becoming instead a vain display of self-righteousness.

In particular, Jesus castigated the use of vain repetitions when praying. He spoke harshly of the practice of heaping up empty phrases when praying supposing one would be heard for their much speaking.

In Greek, the phrase "heap empty phrases" literally means "to babble." (RSV*) "When you pray,"* said Jesus, *"do not keep on babbling [using vain repetitions and heaping empty phrases] like pagans [heathen], for they think that they will be heard for their many words [much speaking]."* (Matthew 6:7)

What Jesus was saying to men of all ages is, "Prayer is communicating with God. Prayer offered for the purpose of calling attention to oneself [whether by where one prays or how one prays] is ostentation."

What impresses God is prayer offered in secret, prayer offered for no reason other than a desire to be *"alone"* with God. *"[Therefore,]"* said Jesus, *"When you pray, [create aloneness with God] go into your room [or*

*a closet] and close the door [that you may be alone with God] and pray to
your Father who is in secret."*

◆　　　◆　　　◆

Jesus also warned against calling attention to one's self when fasting.
(6:16-18). Whether public or private, fasting was intended to be an
experience of joy. Generally, fasts were accompanied by prayer and
supplication and the person fasting wore sackcloth as a sign of penance
and mourning.

Just as men called attention to themselves when praying by offering
prayers in places and in ways that called attention to themselves, they
drew attention to themselves while fasting by wearing a sad, dismal
look on their face, and, in some instances, not washing their face at all.
In the same way men were to avoid calling attention to themselves
when giving their alms and offering their prayers, they were to avoid
even the appearance of fasting by anointing their head and washing
their face.

◆　　　◆　　　◆

When Jesus spoke of hungering and thirsting after righteousness,
He did so knowing His words touched sensitive areas in the lives of
people of the day.

To speak of hungering after righteousness to men for whom food,
clothing, and shelter were daily concerns was certain to capture their
attention. And in speaking of thirsting after righteousness in a land
where the annual rainfall was approximately thirty inches, Jesus
sounded a note with which His listeners were quite familiar.

Unfortunately, in English the full force of the verbs hunger and
thirst do not come through. Normally, in Greek, verbs of hunger and
thirst take the Genitive Case, which implies a person wants part of
something (be it a loaf of bread or a container of water).

In the Fourth Beatitude, however, these verbs are in the Accusative Case the action of which serves to heighten intensity and desire to a level at which men are unwilling to settle for a part of something, but want all there is, be it bread, water, or righteousness.

What Jesus is saying to people of all ages is, "Blessed are those who hunger and thirst for the righteousness of God with an intensity equal to that with which a starving man desires food or a man perishing from a lack of water wants a drink." To be blessed righteousness must become what food is to starving men and water is to men dying from a lack of water.

Righteousness Must Become the Object of Man's Desiring

The righteousness of God is the *summum bonum* or highest good of life. Righteousness is treasure which men and women lay up for themselves in heaven, the lost coin that must be found, the pearl of such great value that those who hunger and thirst willingly sell all they have to possess it.

So, the issue with respect to righteousness is one of desire. "How much do we desire the good things of God? Do we hunger for them with intensity equal to that of a man who is starving or a man who is dying because he has no water?"

From the perspective of desire, the demands of the Fourth Beatitude are as inclusive as the demands of love set forth in Matthew Twenty-Two. To receive the blessing promised in the Beatitude, men must hunger and thirst after the righteousness of God in the same way they are to love: with all their heart, soul, and mind, with all that one is.

The necessity of hungering and thirsting after things spiritual is reflected in Jesus' encounter with the Rich Young Ruler (Matthew 19:16-26).

Disregarding whether the person in question was young (or middle age as some think), what he sought was the spiritual reality of eternal life, and so he asks, *"What must I do?"*

"Obey the commandments," replies Jesus, who then proceeds to name commandments concerning a man's duty to his neighbor.

From all indications, the Young Ruler had lived an exemplary life. *"But, I have kept all these,"* he replies *[meaning I have kept all the commandments named]*, *"What do I lack?"*

If one follows what happens closely, it is apparent that the desire for eternal life is not strong in the Young Ruler, for when Jesus probes the level of his desire by telling him to sell his goods and give the money to the poor, he cannot.

It seems reasonable to suggest that had the Rich, Young Ruler hungered and thirsted after eternal life he would have sold his goods willingly and given the money to relieve the distress of those about him as Jesus requested. As it was, he only wanted eternal life.

Unlike grace, righteousness is not a free gift of God. What Jesus is telling us in this Beatitude is, *"The goodness of God [whether one refers to this goodness as 'righteousness' or 'eternal life'] does not come in wanting, but in hungering and thirsting after it."*

After the Rich, Young Ruler had departed, Jesus took the occasion to comment on how difficult it was for such men to enter the Kingdom of God.

To reap the rewards of business, it was necessary for the camels of businessmen to enter the city by walking through the needle gate on their knees. Yet, as difficult as this maneuver was for camels, it was still easier than for men of wealth and possessions to enter the Kingdom of God because they lacked desire.

It is important to understand Jesus never condemned men simply because they were rich. He spoke harshly of the wealthy because they took advantage of the poor and were unwilling to open their hand to relieve their distress. He spoke critically of them because they were so attached to things of earth that money and possessions became hindrances to seeking the Kingdom of God.

The persistent widow of Luke Eighteen and the friends of the infirm man of Luke Five are studies in what it means to hunger and thirst after something.

What the importuned widow hungered and thirsted for was justice. Addressing the judge, she said, *"Avenge me of mine adversary."*

It is not surprising that a widow should make a request of this kind as they were vulnerable, easily victimized by the powerful and the unscrupulous, especially, if they had no family to provide for them or defend them.

Luke does not identify the widow's adversary. It is possible that this person may have been an unscrupulous tax collector like Zacchaeus. From what historians have said about tax collection during the Roman period and knowledge of the tax burden shouldered by those on the bottom rung of the economic ladder, it is easy to imagine a tax collector as an adversary.

From these comments, if the adversary of the widow had, indeed, been a tax collector, she would have had ample reason to persist in her quest for justice, and on the surface, little to risk should her persistence ruffle the feathers of the judge.

Whatever her cause, as a consequence of hungering and thirsting after justice, the judge agrees to avenge the widow against her adversary, *"...lest by her continual coming she weary me."* (18:5).

◆　　　◆　　　◆

Matthew and Luke record an account of a group of people hungering and thirsting for the healing of a friend.

Jesus is in the city of Capernaum. He has healed many people, among them a leper (Luke 5:12-16) whom He sends on his way with instructions to show himself to the priest and offer the appropriate sacrifice, but not tell anyone about his cleansing.

Disregarding Jesus' instructions, the man proceeds to broadcast the story of his healing and soon the word is out that Jesus is in the area. In time, He is discovered in Peter's home and the people are bringing all manner of diseased and possessed individuals to him.

So many people are gathered in and around Peter's home (Marks says all the entire city was there) that the friends of the infirm man are unable to enter through the door. Undeterred, they climb to the roof, their intention being to remove as much of it as was required to lower their friend into the presence of Jesus.

In the First Century the roofs of homes were made of thatch (saplings overlaid with straw and branches over which clay was spread). When hardened by the sun this mixture made a serviceable covering for homes.

Removing a section of the roof, the friends lower the paralytic into the presence of Jesus. Their persistent hungering and thirsting after the well-being of their friend is rewarded when he is healed.

◆   ◆   ◆

The subtitle assigned the Fourth Beatitude is "The Beatitude of Desire." Examination has established two levels of desire, a level at which humankind wants something and a level at which desire is intense and men hunger and thirst after something.

William Barclay speaks of the intensity of desire involved in hungering and thirsting after righteousness in this way, *"Oh the bliss of the man who longs for total righteousness as a starving man longs for food, and a man perishing of thirst longs for water."*[6]

Understanding the difference involved in wanting something and hungering and thirsting after it, it's important to ask, "What is righteousness? Why are men blessed because they desire hunger and thirst after righteousness rather than just wanting it?"

And, with regard to the blessing promised in the Beatitude, "What did Jesus mean when He said those who hungered and thirsted after righteousness would be filled?"

Righteousness is what humankind must attain to be in right relationship with God. The word that translates righteousness in the Beatitude is *dikaiosuna*. Dikaiosuna has three meanings: (a) justice, (b) right living, and (c) justification.[7]

Part of what is meant by hungering and thirsting after righteousness is to hunger and thirst after justice, to aspire to right living by loving God, neighbor, and self, and to accept all men as if they had never committed an offense.

Righteousness As Justice

Hungering and thirsting after justice may take the course of seeking justice for one's self or others. Some men, Job being a prime example, hunger and thirst after justice for themselves. What they want more than anything else is for everyone to know they are upright regardless of any charge(s) that might be brought against them or circumstances of their lives might suggest.

Job's name means "devoted to God." In the book that bears his name, Job is introduced as a man of unusual integrity. *"There is no one like him,"* says God, *"a perfect and upright man who feareth God and escheweth evil."* (1:8)

Among Jews, righteous men were balanced, well-rounded, and in charge of themselves. In the minds of people they were considered "finished products." Fleming James describes Job the finished product as a man

- Who shunned falsehood and deceit

- Dealt justly toward his servant in any dispute

- With whom the traveler found entertainment or hospitality

- Whose good will extended even to his enemies

- Careful in observing ritual obligations, and

- A man who did not allow his wealth and possessions to come between himself and God.[8]

One day a council of heavenly beings is convened in the presence of God. Satan is there and he openly questions Job's motives in serving God, hinting that Job serves God because it pays.

So Satan is given permission to test Job's faith. *"He is in thine hand,"* says the Lord and in rapid succession, Job's family and possessions are taken from him and Job, himself, is stricken with boils.

Job's misfortunes occasion the visit of three friends, Eliphas, a resident of Teman in Edom, a country renowned for its wisdom; Bildad, whose name means "Beloved of the Lord;" and Zophar, from northwest Arabia.

Job is so disfigured that at first his friends do not recognize him. When they do, they are overcome with grief. They weep, rend their clothes, and sprinkle dust on their heads as if mourning the dead.

After seven days, Eliphas, Bildad, and Zophar begin a round of conversations, the initial thrust of which is to make sense of the misfortune that has fallen upon this ideal, perfect, and upright man. The friends insist Job must have done evil to bring such tragedy and misfortune upon himself. "God is chastising you for your sin." they tell him, "Humble yourself before God, repent, and all will be well again."

Job, however, maintains his innocence. What Job cannot understand is, God being just, why is he—a righteous man—afflicted with such tragedy, misfortune, and adversity? Furthermore, God being a just God, why does He not act on Job's behalf?

From a human perspective, God appears inconsistent and unjust, when supposedly He is Job's champion. What Job yearns for is restoration of the kind of relationship once enjoyed with God.

The Book of Job ends with God speaking to Job out of a whirlwind. In a series of exchanges, God points up Job's lack of wisdom. While

Job cannot fathom the knowledge and power required to create and sustain the world, yet, he has presumed to question God.

Ignoring the charges leveled against Him, God speaks to Job as a friend and moves to restore relationship with him.

Justice for Job comes in restored relationship with God and restoration of all he had lost. Eliphas, Bildad, and Zophar are rebuked and advised to petition Job to intercede on their behalf rather than risk God's wrath.

Justice is served through the setting aside of the doctrine of retribution and the insertion of love in its place.

◆   ◆   ◆

While Job and the importuned widow sought justice for themselves, men and women of the anti-slavery movement in America sought justice for the slave.

It is impossible to pinpoint the origin of slavery. In the Old Testament people became slaves because their land was conquered by another power. Some were enslaved as punishment for theft, others sold themselves into slavery to escape poverty while others became slaves because they were unable to pay their debts. In rare instances, fathers sold their children into servitude. A slave, however, could buy his own freedom, be redeemed by a relative, or be released in the year of Jubilee.

With the rise of Christianity came change. Though Christians continued to make war against each other, they were hesitant to hold each other as slaves.

To the degree that international law existed at the time of exploration of the New World, it opposed the enslavement of Christians. However, as the demand for laborers was heavy and Africa an available source of laborers, Africans were enslaved.

Slavery spread to the English colonies in America in the late Seventeenth Century. Up to the time of its arrival in the colonies, slavery was an exercise of force. In the colonies, it became an exercise of law.

The Christian world being opposed to slavery, missionaries sought to convert slaves to Christianity, which in terms of world sentiment, meant freedom. However, colonial assemblies passed laws changing the basis of slavery from religion to race. Therefore, whether converted or not, persons of African descent remained slaves, children inherited the status of their parents, and slavery became a perpetual institution.

Regrettably, the Constitutional Convention did nothing to abolish slavery. Why that body sidestepped such an important issue is difficult to say. It seems clear that slavery was an economic matter for some members while others believed in the doctrine of biological inequality and racial inferiority. At any rate, the founding fathers left the question of slavery under the constitution indefinite *"...either from fear of alienating the support of two or three states [whose help was needed for ratification of the Constitution]...from utter weariness of a long-sustained struggle for principles...or from the belief that slavery was a decadent institution destined to early extinction."*[9]

The anti-slavery indictment of slavery amounted to a religious crusade at a time when religion played an important role in American life. Appealing to the minds and consciences of men, anti-slavery advocates denounced slavery as a sin, as antithetical to the principles upon which the country was formed, and contrary to both natural and moral law. Slavery, said abolitionists, robbed men created in the image of God of inalienable rights guaranteed them by the Constitution:

- The right to ownership of their bodies
- Freedom of choice as to use of time and to occupation
- The rights of marriage, family, life, and paternal authority
- The right to worship according to conscience

- The right to cultivate their minds, use their peculiar talents and influence their fellow men

- The right to protect themselves, their homes, and their families against violence, and

- The right to the protection of the law.[10]

The dedication of those advocating the abolition of slavery is reflected in the price they paid for seeking justice for slaves. Anti-slavery lecturers were tarred and feathered, beaten, threatened with violence, arrested and cast into jail. Many broke under the strain of their experience. Abolitionist clergymen were censured for their beliefs. Many found churches closed to them. Some were ostracized by their families.

James Gillespie Birney, Theodore Weld, and Angelina Grimke are examples of the men and women who paid the price for seeking justice for the slave. Birney, prominent attorney in Huntsville, Alabama, and former slave holder, was forced to leave his native state of Kentucky when a mob gathered to destroy *The Olive Branch*, the anti-slavery newspaper he published. Later, his father warned him against returning to Kentucky even for a visit.[11]

Weld, a pastor's son, born in Connecticut and reared in western New York, lectured widely for the abolition of slavery, though his meetings were generally mobbed. Eventually, physically exhausted from his efforts, Weld lost his voice.[12]

Angelina Grimke, daughter of a member of the South Carolina Supreme Court, lectured and wrote against slavery on the basis that

- Slavery was hereditary and perpetual

- Slave labor was compulsory and uncompensated

- Slaves could be sold or leased

- Slave families ruthlessly separated

- Slaves could not testify against a white man in court
- Salves could be punished at will, and finally,
- That there was no way by which they could redeem themselves.

Her pamphlet, *Appeal to the Christian Woman of the South*, created such a furor that postmasters burned it publicly. Forced to flee her home in South Carolina and threatened with mob violence should she return, Angelina traveled North where she became an agent of the American Anti-Slavery Society, paying her own expenses and drawing no salary.[13]

◆   ◆   ◆

Hungering and thirsting after righteousness, men and women not only seek justice for themselves as Job did, or justice for others as Americans, North and South, did on behalf of the slave, some hunger and thirst after righteousness understood as the good life.

Righteousness understood as the good life is living one's life in accordance with God's standard on a personal level, and on an inter-personal level, living it in a way that promotes peace and well-being among people.

On a personal level, the man who pursues righteousness understood as the good life is balanced, well-rounded, and in charge of himself. He is genuine, authentic, and real. His exterior and interior speak the same truth. His word is his bond. In both public and private areas of life, the man who hungers and thirsts after righteousness promotes peace and well-being.

The third meaning of righteousness is justification.

To be justified is to be counted as righteous before God. Theologians speak of the "fall of man," as the point at which humankind departed from the Purpose of God and sin entered human living. Having departed from God's Intent, man can do nothing to atone for his sinfulness, nothing to merit the removal of guilt. Powerless to pay for his sin he remains under condemnation until justified by God.

In the modern world when a person transgresses the law, if proven guilty, he is assigned a penalty, usually in the form of a specified amount of money, or for more serious crimes, time in jail or prison. When that penalty is paid, the offender is freed from condemnation under the law.

Warrants are destroyed. Guilt is removed. A right relationship with society is restored.

The Protestant reformer Martin Luther struggled with the issue of justification for much of his life. He was filled with religious doubts concerning his salvation because he did not feel justified before God.

Luther sought, unsuccessfully, to remove his doubts by following the established practices of the Church. It was not until he began working on a series of lectures on the Book of Romans that Luther's doubts were put to rest. In Romans, he read, *"The just shall live by faith."* Man is justified by faith in God. He is counted as righteous because of his faith.

◆   ◆   ◆

Having examined Jesus' words, *"Blessed are they who hunger and thirst after righteousness,"* how are we to understand the blessing promised in the Fourth Beatitude that those who hunger and thirst after righteousness *"will be filled?"*

William Barclay sheds light on this phrase by noting that the word translated "filled" was used *originally "…to describe the special fattening of animals for killing."* When applied to men, however, it means *"to stuff a person to the point of complete satiety."*[14] In other words, it is in hungering and thirsting after righteousness that man is filled, stuffed to the point at which he can hold no more of the good he seeks, namely, the righteousness of God.

Notes To Shepherds

To be a good shepherd, men and women must hunger and thirst after whatever makes them effective and potent in their calling.

As is the case with all vocations, however, there are occupational hazards to be avoided. One hazard encountered in shepherding human sheep is that of one's ego becoming so inflated that the role of shepherd becomes a platform for calling attention to one's self.

Shepherds with inflated egos cease listening and responding to the voice that called them. They separate themselves from the very people they have been called to serve. They cease giving themselves in a potent manner to meeting the needs of the sheep in their care. They lose a sense of the flock.

At this juncture, it is perhaps as difficult to be a shepherd as any time in history. Affluence, mobility, professionalism, and technology are exerting strong influences upon shepherd and sheep alike.

Yet, at the same time, one cannot deny the hunger and thirst pervading society and its people for meaning, purpose, and direction. Subject to the tugs and pulls, pressures and temptations present in a technologically driven society, members of the human flock are asking, "What saith the Lord, shepherd? How am I to live victoriously on the streets of the city I live in? Roots that once anchored my life are disappearing. Is there a word from God?"

At a time when forces threaten to push people beyond their bounds of adaptability, human sheep are hungry for the good things of God, hungry for sermons that increase their knowledge of Scripture and assure them God's ear remains open and his arms extended.

In a society whose people sit four to five hours in subfreezing weather to watch a football game, members of the household of God are looking for more than a one point, fifteen minute "make me feel good sermon" on Sunday morning.

Sheep hungry and thirsty for the good things of God will find time for prayer and bible study and will give their time, their talents, and their money in support of worthy ministries.

Perhaps, what is needed is for shepherds to ask themselves, "Have I lost the joy of being a servant?" One thing is certain. As long as the joy of service is missing from the lives of shepherds, human sheep will not have everything they need. Until human sheep have everything they need, they will not lie down, because they cannot.

7

Oh the Blessedness
of the Merciful

✦

The Beatitude
of Loving-Kindness

I n *Jerusalem, One City, Three Faiths*, Karen Armstrong discusses the
tendency of Christ's followers to develop "sacred geography" as an
adjunct to worship.[1]

Sacred geography is not geography in the usual sense of the word. It
is best described as a landscape of spiritual symbols and concepts that
awaken in us a sense of the presence of God, contribute to a deeper
understanding of God, and encourage a more comprehensive expression of faith when appropriated into the lives of people.

◆   ◆   ◆

Mercy is the concept around which Jesus weaves the Fourth Beatitude. From the perspective of a society in the throes of transition,
mercy *is "a refraining from harming or punishing offenders, enemies, persons in one's power; kindness in excess of what may be expected or
demanded by fairness…"*[2] To be merciful is to exhibit *"the disposition to
forgive, pity, or be kind."*[3]

The word that translates mercy most frequently in the Old Testament is *hesed.* Hesed is *"mercy, loving-kindness, love, loyalty, and faithfulness."*[4]

"Hesed," writes William Barclay, *"means the ability to get right inside the other person's skin until we can see things with his eyes, think things with his mind, and feel things with his feelings."*[5]

All of these thoughts come together in the New Testament where mercy is *eleos,* the general meaning of which is, *"To have compassion or mercy on a person in unhappy circumstances,"* implying a *"feeling for the misfortunes of others...but also an active desire to remove those miseries."*[6]

Mercy understood as sacred geography is empathic as well as relational in character. To be merciful is to have compassion for persons whose situations are unhappy and whose circumstances are unfortunate. It implies a willingness to be actively and directly involved in the lives of people, helping to improve their situations and change the unfortunate nature of their circumstances.

It was in the Temple at Jerusalem during the final week of His earthly ministry that Jesus gave the *Parable of the Good Samaritan,* His most comprehensive teaching on the subject of mercy.

In Luke, the Parable is given in response to questions raised by an attorney. Echoing the words of the Rich, Young Ruler, the attorney asks, *"What must I do to inherit eternal life?"* to which Jesus responds, *"What is written in the Law? How do you read it?"*

"Love the Lord with all your heart, and with all your soul, and with all your strength, and with all your mind, and love your neighbor as yourself" replies the attorney.

"Do this," said Jesus, *"[love in these areas in the manner suggested] and you will live."*

Then, because his blind spot is relational rather than material (as was the case with the Rich, Young Ruler), and wanting to test Jesus, the attorney asks, *"And who is my neighbor?"*

◆   ◆   ◆

While the motive of the attorney is questionable, nonetheless, he raises issues with which people of all ages have grappled, namely, *"What is love?" and "Who is my neighbor?"*

These important issues are addressed in the *Parable of the Good Samaritan.*

Set against a background of difficult relationships, it is easy for the central truth of the Parable, namely, the Samaritan's demonstration of mercy to a stranger to get lost.

In addition, it is easy to gloss over the fact that in recognizing the wounded traveler as his "neighbor" and showing him mercy, the Samaritan hurdled cultural, religious, and social prejudices as strong as any with which Americans have struggled since the birth of this nation.

Following the death of Solomon, the Kingdom of Israel divided into a Northern Kingdom (sometimes called Israel, sometimes Samaria, with its capital at the city of Samaria), and a Southern Kingdom (called Judah with its capital at Jerusalem).

Less than three hundred years later, both kingdoms are overrun by foreign nations, the Northern Kingdom falling to the Assyrians in 722-21 BC, and Judah, the Southern Kingdom, succumbing to the Babylonians one hundred and thirty years later.

◆   ◆   ◆

In the ancient world, it was the policy of conquering nations to identify individuals and groups in the population of a vanquished country who might prove troublesome, and deport these people to the land of their conquerors.

With regard to the Northern Kingdom, nearly twenty-eight thousand persons were deported to Assyria where, for all intents and purposes, they disappeared from the stream of human history.[7] Left in the land were the lowest, the poorest, and the least educated elements of the population.

Jews left in the land proved so troublesome and rebellious that Assyria initiated a systematic program aimed at strengthening Assyrian presence and weakening Jewish identity.

They implemented this policy by bringing colonists from all parts of Assyria and settling them in what had once been the Northern King-dom (2 Kings 17:24). Taking the name Samaritan from the area in which they were placed, these colonists settled down, eventually inter-marrying with Jews left in the land. From this merging of blood streams would come the people called Samaritans and upon the return of the exiles from Babylonia, centuries of strife and hardship between Jews and Samaritans.

Difficulties developed along lines of blood and religion. Because they were people of mixed blood, the Samaritans were ridiculed as half-breeds and foreigners by Jews of the Exile.

Because their priests had been included in the deportation and wor-ship of Jehovah so attenuated in the years preceding the downfall of Israel, it was necessary for people left in the land to sent for priests to *"teach them the rituals of the god of the land."* (2 Kings 17:27) Thereaf-ter, the Samaritans worshiped the God of Israel, retaining belief in God as Creator and basing their religious practices on the books of Moses. With the passing of time the Samaritans came to consider themselves orthodox in their faith.

Thinking themselves orthodox, the Samaritans wanted to help rebuild the Temple at Jerusalem (520-515 BC). When their offer is rejected, they tried to prevent completion of the project (most likely by blocking the importation of lumber and other building materials).

Returning from Babylonia some eighty years after the completion of the Temple, Ezra the priest did little to improve relations between Samaritans and Jews.

Finding the core or "holy seed" of the community (including the priests and Levites) had intermarried with the people of the land, Ezra initiated a harsh, uncompromising program of reform which included the establishment of a divorce court (with himself as the judge). Jews who had married Samaritan women were compelled to "put them away," that is, divorce their wives, an action that brought untold suffering to the lives of many innocent women and children. (Ezra 10:17-44). Later, marriage between Jews and non-Jews was prohibited altogether (Nehemiah 13:23-20).

The final break between Jews and Samaritans came when, prohibited from worshiping at the temple at Jerusalem, Samaritans built a rival temple on Mount Gerizim, claiming Shechem rather than Jerusalem as the true "Beth-el" or "House of God," the site traditionally chosen and blessed by the Lord, the place where Jehovah had put His name.

◆   ◆   ◆

In the Parable of the Good Samaritan, however, relations between Jews and Samaritans is not an issue. The traveler waylaid on the road is not identified as a Jew (although one might presume he was) and the name of the Samaritan is never given.

Therefore, as far at the Parable is concerned, the answer to the question, "Who is my neighbor," would seem to be "anyone who needs my help."

Interestingly enough, apart from the Fourth Beatitude, Jesus makes no reference to mercy. He comes closest to the subject by echoing Micah who said what the Lord required of men was that they should *"do justly, and to love mercy, and to walk humbly"* before their God. (Micah 6:8)

◆   ◆   ◆

What was it then that earned the Samaritan the title of *"Good?"* What was it that set him apart from the priest and Levite on the road that day? Why did the Samaritan stop and help a total stranger while the Priest and Levite elected to "pass by on the other side?"

The Samaritan is called "good" for several reasons. He was the only person on the road conscious of the bond linking them to the man who had fallen among thieves, the only one moved by compassion to become involved in alleviating the misery of a stranger.

While one might have anticipated the priest or Levite to aid the beleaguered man, neither did. Neither stopped because neither had the ability to get inside the skin of the injured man. Neither felt compassion for him as if his situation were their own.

The Samaritan is called "good" because upon finding a traveler stripped of his clothes and left for dead, the Samaritan becomes involved in alleviating his misery, binding up the man's wounds, and as oil and wine were thought to have curative properties, pouring oil and wine on them.

He is called "good" as well for, having done everything possible, he sets the wounded man upon his own beast and transports him to an inn, where Luke says, he *"took care of him."* (10:34)

The next morning, before continuing his journey, the Samaritan leaves money with the innkeeper for the care of the wounded man, promising upon his return to reimburse the innkeeper for any additional expense incurred.

One feature of the Parable easily overlooked is that the man on the road could only trigger in those passing by what was already in them. There is a truth which says, "Nothing can get out of you that is not already in you." The Samaritan responded to the wounded man because compassion was in him, whereas, the Priest and Levite did not because compassion was not in them.

The Samaritan responded as he did because he saw the situation of the wounded man as if it were his own, as if he, himself, had been wounded, stripped of his clothes, and left for dead. It is as if in conversation with himself that day, the Samaritan said, "If I were in this man's shoes, I would need someone to come along who, seeing me stripped of my clothes and left for dead would have compassion, stop, bind up my wounds, and take me to a place where I could rest in safety."

Who Are the Merciful?

So who are the merciful? What behaviors characterize those who show compassion to others? And why are the merciful blessed in the way they are?

Earlier we saw that the general meaning of mercy was, *"To have compassion or mercy on a person in unhappy circumstances,"* implying a *"feeling for the misfortunes of others…but also an active desire to remove those miseries."*

"Compassion," as Bill Blackburn reminds us, comes from two Latin words—*com,* meaning "with," and *pati,* meaning "suffer."[8] Compassion is the capacity to suffer with another person, the ability to enter the situation and circumstance of another so completely that the fate of the one showing compassion and the one receiving it, are linked.

The merciful feel the pain of others because they suffer with them. They identify with those whose situations and circumstances are difficult. They actively seek to alleviate the misery of the unfortunate, improve their situation, and infuse them with courage because that is what they, themselves, would need in similar circumstances.

Aware of their own sins and desiring to grow in wholeness and completeness, the merciful commit themselves to meeting the needs and acting in the best interests of their neighbors, even when these people are strangers.

In short, the merciful are men and women who love the people God loves in the way God loves them, demonstrating in their lives and relationships the loving-kindness, mercy, and compassion of God.

Having identified the merciful, it seems equally important to note who the merciful are not.

To begin, the merciful are neither pushovers nor rescuers, wimps, or easy touches. They resist the temptation to rescue or take responsibility for the lives of others, focusing instead, on infusing neighbors in unfortunate situations with nutrient and integrative power.[9]

Nutrient power is the energy of compassion. Compassion nourishes and promotes growth any time one person says to another, "I care about you," and demonstrates this fact by addressing a given circumstance or situation in the same way the Samaritan addressed that of the wounded man on the road.

Integrative power is power added to that of another person when additional power is needed. Rather than impede the growth of others by rescuing them, the merciful add their power to that of individuals in unfortunate situations and circumstances, making them stronger.

We do not show mercy to our neighbor by rescuing them. Rescuing is taking responsibility for the life of another person. Once assumed, responsibility for another is a burden difficult to relinquish as those who abdicate responsibility for their lives are hesitant to take it up again. It is at the point of being unable to rid themselves of their burden that rescuers understand themselves victims of their own misguided compassion.

The present situation in the area of welfare speaks volumes on how ill-advised it is to rescue others. Americans are generous people. Since the days of the Great Depression, agencies of the government and segments of the private sector have extended a helping hand to people in difficult circumstances.

Because misguided administrations and societal agencies have confused rescuing with being merciful, we live in a society victimized by its own good intentions. Rather than remaining an expression of compassion on the part of society for its less fortunate members, welfare is claimed as a right not only by the unfortunate, but by those unwilling to work.

Rather than rescuing people and eventually becoming a victim of one's caring, why not infuse people with the power they need to move forward, power that encourages personal growth. Then, should people choose not to grow, love them enough to leave them where they are.

◆   ◆   ◆

So, what did Jesus mean when he said, *"Blessed are the merciful for they shall obtain mercy?"* In what way is mercy the reward of the merciful?

Mercy, it seems, is its own reward. Those who show mercy will be shown mercy. Those who demonstrate compassion will be shown compassion.

According to the editor of *Hastings Dictionary of the Bible,* mercy traced through ecclesiastical Latin carries the idea of "reward."[10] When an alms giver opened his heart and extended his hand to someone less fortune than he, the one receiving the alms often rewarded their benefactor by pronouncing a blessing upon them. "May God reward you in heaven," is an appropriate blessing. In effect, "God bless you."[11]

The blessing promised in the merciful in the Beatitude is the very thing they have given others: compassion, loving-kindness, faithfulness, and loyalty.

Notes for Shepherds

While in the popular mind, the role of shepherd is generally reserved for professional clergymen, in the biblical sense, everyone is a shepherd of some flock.

Parents are shepherds as are employers. And whether one identifies their flock as the congregation of a church, members of one's family, or employees of one's business, to be blessed shepherds are to demonstrate mercy and compassion.

To be numbered among the merciful, it is essential that shepherds

- Understand that as all men have the same range of life experiences, at some time everyone stands in need of compassion

- Dedicate themselves to doing whatever is required to become a finished product, balanced, in control of one's self, master of one's spirit

- Develop the capacity to identify the needs of people and commit to meeting those needs

- Understand that mercy requires compassion and compassion requires action.

In short, to be numbered among the merciful, shepherds must exhibit the strengths of those blessed by God in the Beatitudes studied thus far:

- The trust demonstrated by the poor in spirit

- The sensitivity and compassion of those who mourn the difficulty, calamity, and loss their neighbors are experiencing

- The self-control and self-mastery of the meek

- The intense desire of those who hunger and thirst for righteousness.

While it is dangerous to engage in global generalities, it is exciting to imagine what life would be like if a larger segment of the world's population modeled their lives after the Samaritan. If a larger percentage of people were as compassionate to their neighbor(s) as the Samaritan was to the man on the road to Jericho, would not society and its people be more sensitive and compassionate?

Would not a greater percentage of the world's people be inwardly a bit more secure and confident in themselves than they are at present?

Would they not be more in control of and master of themselves?

Would not the drive to do what is right, good, and best become so strong that people everywhere would be convinced the more we love the more we are loved in return?

Would we not be more appreciative and respectful of the humanity of others, more understanding when others express thoughts and act in ways that run against the grain of our personal lives?

Would we not be reminded that "but for the grace of God" we might all be numbered among the poor, the suffering, the sorrowful, and the lawless?

8

Oh the Blessedness
of the Pure in Heart

◆

The Beatitude of Attitude

From the Creation of the world until the entrance of sin into human living, the Bible presents humankind (represented by Adam and Eve) as people whose motives are pure. If, as is widely held, Adam can represent an individual or the entire human race, then it can be said that until the entrance of sin the motives of humankind were unmixed. God communed daily with Adam and Eve. In turn, they were comfortable relating with their Creator because their motives were beyond question.

With the entrance of sin, however, mixed motives became a factor in human living.

Motives determine the quality of all human relationships. When motives are mixed, it is hard for persons to connect with each other in friendship as each must determine whether the agenda of the other is honorable or dishonorable.

◆ ◆ ◆

Jesus intended the Beatitudes function as behavioral guidelines for disciples and citizens of the Kingdom of God. The standard they set for human conduct is high, leaving no room for mixed motives.

The Sixth Beatitude calls for disciples and citizens of the Kingdom to be "pure in heart." To understand what Jesus intended requires examining the concept of purity in both the Old and New Testaments, determining how purity is acquired, and ascertaining what Jesus meant when He said the pure in heart would *"see God."*

◆   ◆   ◆

Purity is an important subject in both Old and New Testaments. The word translated "pure" in the Septuagint as well as the New Testament is *katharos.* Though capable of a variety of meanings and applications, the basic meaning of katharos is *"unmixed, unadulterated, unalloyed, uncontaminated, that is, clean, without blemish or imperfection."*[1]

To be pure in heart man must be unmixed in his motives, unadulterated in his thoughts, uncontaminated in his attitude, and unalloyed in his behavior. Pure in heart, without blemish or imperfection, man is balanced, in control, master of himself, a finished product pleasing to God.

◆   ◆   ◆

Two concepts of purity dominated the thinking of people in the time of Christ.

The Scribes and Pharisees ascribed to ceremonial purity obtained by refraining from things forbidden by the Law or observing rituals and ceremonies endorsed in the Law.

Jesus, on the other hand, advocated moral and spiritual purity, a state of being—mind and heart—acquired by living a life of integrity, uprightness, and innocence in relationship with God.[2]

John's account of the woman taken in adultery demonstrates the views of Jesus and the religious leaders of Israel on the subject of purity. (John 8:1-11)

◆ ◆ ◆

Returning to Jerusalem from the Mount of Olives early one morning, Jesus enters the Temple and begins to teach.

John's Gospel does not inform us what Jesus' subject was that morning nor where He was in the Temple. However, as it is religious leaders who bring the woman into the Temple area, we can assume Jesus was in or near the Court of the Women.

To appreciate the situation we need to remember Jesus has entered upon the last week of His life. Men opposed to Jesus are searching for some excuse to seize Him.

The drama unfolds in this manner. The Scribes and Pharisees approach bringing a woman whom they say has been taken in the very act of adultery. Setting her in the midst of those present, they say to Jesus, *"Master, this woman was caught in the act of adultery."*

Assuming the people who had been listening to Jesus did not disperse immediately, a small crowd would have been present to witness Jesus' encounter with some of Israel's religious leaders.

Opposition to Jesus is the most likely explanation for the Scribes and Pharisees joining together to bring the woman to Jesus. Their coming, however, is suspect on several grounds.

First, their use of "Master" in addressing Jesus was inappropriate as that was a form of greeting used by disciples to address the teacher with whom they had identified, whose teachings they had accepted as authoritative for their lives, to whom they had pledged their loyalty and obedience.

Addressing a teacher as "Master," disciples said to the world, *"We have linked our fate with the fate of this man."*

Peter's response to his act of denial can be attributed, in part, to the fact that having identified with Jesus, accepted Jesus' teachings as authoritative for his life, and pledged loyalty and obedience to him, Peter had, in effect, linked his fate to that of Christ. It could be that the intensity with which Peter attempted to dissociate himself from Jesus in Pilate's courtyard, going so far as to deny he even knew him, can be attributed to the fact that in his mind Peter felt he might be required to share Jesus' fate.

As the Scribes and Pharisees had neither identified with Jesus, pledged loyalty to Him, nor accepted His teachings as authoritative for their lives, their use of "Master" as a form of address suggests their motive for bringing the woman to Jesus is something other than what they present it as being.

Secondly, it isn't clear in what capacity the Scribes and Pharisees are acting in bringing the woman.

If acting in a legal capacity, that is, intent upon leveling a charge of adultery against the woman, the presence of the man with whom she had committed adultery (adultery being a crime against society as well as a punishable offense) would have been required.

Thirdly, if their concern was the behavior of the woman, adultery being a serious crime, a charge of adultery would more appropriately have been presented in the Hall of Hewn Stones where the proceedings of the highest court in Judaism, the Sanhedrin, were held. As some of them were probably members of the Sanhedrin, there was no need to bring her to Jesus at all.

Whether operating in a legal or non-official capacity, how could the Scribes and Pharisees have known an act of adultery was taking place? What information would they have needed to catch the woman in the very act of adultery?

All things considered, the coming of the Scribes and Pharisees smacks of a "setup." Thus, the directness of their words. *"Master, this woman was caught in the act of adultery. In the Law Moses commanded us to stone such women. Now what do you say? What should be done with her?"*

Among the Hebrews, the Law was the most sacred part of the Hebrew Bible. Jews honored the Law as the measuring stick by which one determined whether things were authoritative and inspired or not.[3]

Because Jews of the First Century did not divide life into religious and secular spheres as we do in contemporary society, what the Law had to say on a given subject constituted the Will of God. In other words, the Law integrated theology and psychology as it was assumed what a man believed would be reflected in his conduct. Further, it was believed, as the Law came from God who, Himself, was holy, righteous, and good, it was binding on the people and God would uphold it.[4]

The question which the Scribes and Pharisees ask regarding adultery and the Law is blatantly cryptic as they knew Jesus was versed in the Law, therefore, as aware as they, that under the Law adultery was a crime the penalty for which was death by stoning.

Stoning was a form of capital punishment in Israel. Usually, stoning took place outside the city walls in the presence of witnesses and members of the community with witnesses against the accused casting the first stones. Then, as stoning was an offense against the entire community, members of the community also cast stones.[5]

It seems obvious that the motive for bringing the woman to Jesus had little to do with upholding the Law or purifying the moral climate of society. In all likelihood, the objective of the Scribes and Pharisees was to maneuver Jesus into a position in which He could be accused of disregarding the Law or taking some step that would bring Him into conflict with Roman authorities.

If Jesus says, "Stone her," He can be charged with illegally inciting others to kill, a charge certain to come to the attention of the Roman authorities who had withheld from Jews the right to put a person to death. On the other hand, if Jesus does not pass sentence upon the woman, then He can be accused of condoning adultery (which would discredit Him in the eyes of the people for whom adultery was a crime against society deserving of stoning).

Two options were open to Jesus. Respond to the cryptic question concerning adultery or pass judgment upon the woman.

Jesus does neither. Instead, He stoops down and begins to write on the ground with His finger, something people did when they wanted to give the impression of being preoccupied or wished to be deliberately inattentive.

In light of the fact that their attempt at discrediting Jesus had not succeeded, coupled with the fact that He said nothing, and by writing on the ground was deliberately inattentive to people used to commanding attention, the silence that followed must have been particularly awkward.

When they continue pressing Him for an answer, Jesus stands and says to the Scribes and Pharisees, *"He that is without sin cast the first stone."* Then once more, he resumed writing on the ground.

It is interesting to speculate what Jesus wrote. If, as the text says, the woman was in the midst of the crowd, it is possible she was the only person in position to see what Jesus was writing. In view of her display of courage at a time when her life was literally in the balance, it may be that Jesus wrote words that give her courage to conduct herself with dignity.

Let's pause and look at the several factions present.

First, the Accusers

Scribes and Pharisees, religious leaders of Israel willing to expose a woman to public humiliation for the purpose of maneuvering an adversary into a position in which they could accuse Him of disregarding the Law or violating some aspect of relationship with Rome.

Next, the Accused

Her name is never given. She endures the shame and humiliation of public accusation without uttering a word. She makes no attempt at rationalizing her behavior. Nor does she endeavor to displace blame for her actions onto others or cop out on the environment. She knows she has sinned and that she deserves to be stoned under the Law.

Finally, the Advocate

In effect, by refusing to respond to the question posed by the Scribes and Pharisees or pass sentence upon the woman, what Jesus has done is elevate the encounter to a higher, more honest, level.

At the level of having committed adultery for which stoning was the appropriate punishment, perhaps, no one except the woman was guilty. As witnesses to the woman's adultery, the Scribes and Pharisees would have been first to cast stones.

No stone would be cast, however, for at the level of being without sin, all were guilty.

The end of the matter is this. John writes, *"But they having heard, and by their conscience being convicted, went out one by one, beginning from the elder ones until the last."*

Left alone with the woman and there being no accusers, Jesus says to her, *"Has no one condemned you? Then neither do I. Go now and leave your life of sin."*

◆   ◆   ◆

Having examined views of purity prominent in the First Century, what did Jesus have in mind when He declared blessed those who were pure in heart? And what did Jesus mean when He indicated the pure in heart would see God?

A short comment on Hebrew psychology is needed to answer these questions. Hebrews thought of the heart as the personal center of man. As Hebrew psychology permitted one part of the body to stand for the total person, nearly all of the references to heart in the Old Testament are to personality as a whole, the inner life, or the character of a person.[6]

In the Gospels, the heart is pictured as soil in which moral seed grows in the same way seed grows in the physical world. When these seeds take root they are manifested as uprightness in character, thoughts, feelings, attitudes, and actions.

Therefore, when Jesus spoke of the pure in heart, He had in mind individuals of exemplary personality and character, persons of integrity, clear conscience, and singleness of purpose, individuals devoid of low aims and mixed motives who had detached from earth and things of earth and placed their trust in God.

◆   ◆   ◆

"Blessed are those whose entire personality, inner life, and character is pure, for they shall see God."

Men in the ancient world knew no greater privilege nor could they imagine an honor greater than that of being in the presence of the king who, together with his wives, children, personal servants, and members of his harem lived in a royal palace surrounded by a host of officials and attendants known as men of the king's presence.[7]

Included among those who routinely came into the presence of the king was the Minister of the Palace or Royal Steward, the Royal Secretary, and the Royal Herald.

Each of these men wore a distinctive robe and were assigned specific duties such as unlocking the gate to the king's palace, attending to the royal correspondence, and tending to those seeking an audience with the king.[8]

◆   ◆   ◆

In the same way, standing in the king's presence was the highest honor imaginable in the ancient world, the high honor assured the pure in heart is that they will see God.

Yet, God is not seen with the naked eye as Moses discovered. When he expressed a desire to see the glory of Jehovah, Moses was told no one could see God and live. When the High Priest entered the Holy of Holies on the Day of Atonement, he created a cloud of smoke by pouring water upon hot coals that he might not look upon the presence of God.

We do see God through eyes of faith, however. To see Him is to know Him, to know His truth, and experience His presence. To see God is to affirm His presence in the experiences of life—regardless of their nature—working for good that we might be more like His Son. To see him is to view His Creation and see His witness there.

Notes for Shepherds

Shepherding human flocks is a vocation to which men and women are called when addressed by the voice of God. Persons who respond affirmatively have a strong sense of being in the right place doing what they are intended to do. They feel important, valued, and needed, thus what they do is a source of joy.

While it sometimes happens that individuals not called by God function as shepherds, they do not derive the same joy from what they do as those who know themselves called to shepherd human sheep.

Purity of heart must be the goal of all who shepherd human sheep. They must strive to live lives characterized by rightness of mind and relationship toward God and singleness of purpose with regard to seeking His Kingdom.

In *The Be-Happy Attitudes*, Robert Schuller suggests a four-step process for acquiring purity of heart. Men and women become pure in heart by (a) Wising up, (b) Cleaning up, (c) Giving up, and (d) Taking up.[9]

Shepherds become pure in heart by wising up to the reality that they have been called to give themselves to something higher, greater, and purer than themselves. Theirs is a high and holy calling requiring them to live in the world, love it not, yet overcome it.

Shepherds progress toward purity of heart by cleaning up, removing, or ridding themselves of any trait, characteristic, or behavior that might cast doubt upon their calling or blemish their image as a shepherd. Anything short of purity limits the effectiveness of the shepherd in the same way dirt on the lens of reading glasses restricts the ability of the wearer to discern the words of a newspaper or telephone book.

Impurity in the life of shepherds is ultimately detected as a lessening of potency in the care and management of human sheep. Impurity prompts shepherds to give preferential treatment to some members of the flock, recognize the contributions of certain members, neglect the contributions of others, and limit the service opportunities of some members of the congregation.

In a larger sense, however, because each flock has but one shepherd, and the well-being of the flock is tied so closely to this person, shepherds who hunger and thirst to be pure in heart can ill-afford anything that smacks of impurity if sheep in their care are to know abundant life.

◆   ◆   ◆

The thing that stands out above all else in this Beatitude is the blessing of seeing God is limited to those who are pure in heart. What this means for shepherds is their theology and their psychology must square if they are to be effective in their service.

In English, theology is a combination of two Greek words, *Theos*,[10] which means "God," and *logos*, which is usually translated as "word" or "meaning."[11] The meaning of these words is beautifully expressed in the Prologue to John's Gospel.

When John declares, *"In the beginning was the word, and the word was with God, and the word was God,"* what he is doing is defining theology as the truth of God, the truth about God, and the truth that enables us to know God.

Our word psychology comes from a similar combination of words, *psuche*, which means "principle of life,"[12] and *logos*, which again means "word." Psychology is the truth of man and the truth about man. It enables man to "understand himself, interpret his actions, and correct, change, or alter his thoughts and behavior."

To the extent that the theology of men is sound and their psychology is healthy, they are pure in heart as the truth of their life and the truth about their life reflect the same reality.

When the theology of shepherds does not speak the same truth as their psychology, the tendency is to hide behind one's role, draw theological boxes, rehearse a denominational position, insist on a given interpretation of Scripture, or unable to give an answer to some of the difficult questions people ask, to fall back on the hackneyed phrase, "Have faith, brother," which in most instances means, "I don't know."

It is essential that shepherds commit themselves to whatever is required for their theology and psychology to square. One step in that direction taken by some is the practice of seeking a spiritual advisor whose maturity and experience qualify them to shepherd shepherds.

As growth rather than perfection is the goal of the shepherd, if the person selected as spiritual advisor is trained in psychology as well as theology, so much the better as it is essential to address any issue, situation, circumstance, or behavior that stands in the way of the shepherd's ability to give himself or herself in a potent manner to the care and management of sheep.

A recommended second step would be for shepherds to ask the Spirit of God to walk through the many rooms of their life, cleansing each as it moves until all shine with the purity of God-likeness.

Essentially, anything negative—be it thought, feeling, or deed—constitutes impurity and makes the shepherd less effective. To be effective in their calling, shepherds need to be as free as possible of doubt or guilt, hostility or frustration, depression or despair, fear, worry, addiction, or resentment, as with these things in their lives it is like "seeing through a mirror darkly," rather than "face to face."

In the third place, to be pure in heart shepherds need to *"give up"* anything that inhibits, hampers, or impedes relationship with God, anything that takes God's rightful place in their life or relegates the Kingdom of God to second place in their scale of values. Anything that stands between the shepherd and God is an indication of impurity for which shepherds cannot be blessed.

Finally, to be pure in heart, shepherds need to take up their Cross, some good work, cause, or purpose that will improve the lot of human-kind.

9

Oh the Blessedness
of the Peacemakers

◆

The Beatitude
of World Conditioning

A s He journeyed toward Jerusalem on what was to be His last visit
to that city, Jesus began preparing the disciples for what lay ahead,
namely that He would be delivered into the hands of sinners and
would lay down His life as a sacrifice.

Knowing these disclosures evoked fear and apprehension in men He
had chosen as His disciples, Jesus sought to comfort them by bestowing peace upon them and speaking of the coming of the Comforter.
"My peace, I leave with you, my peace I give unto you."

But, what did Jesus mean when He spoke of His peace? What is the
nature of the peace He identified as His? In what way, if any, does the
peace Jesus said He was leaving differ from the peace the world gives?

Assuming there is a difference, how do those who aspire to be
known as children of God go about cultivating the peace of God in
their own lives and the lives of those with whom they come into contact?

◆   ◆   ◆

In the opinion of many biblical scholars, peace is a concept distinctly peculiar to Christianity, a concept as rich in meaning as it is broad in scope. In the Old Testament, peace is personal and social well-being. In the broadest sense, peace is *shalom*.

Since ancient times, whether encountering or taking leave of each other, Jews have communicated their wishes and intentions by means of a blessing of shalom, because incorporated in shalom are ideas and concepts that convey meaning, wholeness, serenity, security, health, well-being, and prosperity.[1]

By means of the shalom blessing Jews wished each other peace, understood as *"everything that contributes to contentment in life, everything that works for your good, everything that contributes to your well-being, everything that promotes tranquility, well-being, and order in life."*[2]

In the New Testament the Greek word *eirana* translates the Hebrew shalom. Eirana is inner peace, a state of being characterized by wholeness, tranquility, and contentment in all areas of life, including relationships.[3] Peace is the inner state of a person who enjoys what Augustine described as "tranquility of order."[4]

Repeatedly, in the salutations of his letters, Paul spoke of peace to fellow laborers in Christ. To the Corinthians, Ephesians, Philippians, Colossians, Thessalonians, and Timothy, Paul wrote, *"Grace and peace be to you from God our Father and the Lord Jesus Christ."* (I Corinthians 1:3)

We experience something of Jesus' peace when moved by a beautiful sunset, the roar of a great river (such as the Niagara where it empties into Niagara Falls), by the wind as it moves through a grove of trees, or when, as happens to couples committed to each other, one of them awakens during the night and is overwhelmed by the meaning their sleeping mate has for them.

We experience inner peace as well in the infant that sleeps in our arms, the performance of great music, when we give ourselves selflessly to others, or make sacrifices that life might be better for those about us with no thought of getting anything in return.

We experience the peace of God any time we connect spirit-to-spirit with another person. Connected in this way, people are free to experience fellowship, communicate, and relate, each person experiencing the warmth of relationship knowing they are loved for no reason other than they are who they are.

In contrast to the peace of God, peace as the world understands it is the absence of tension and conflict. Peace defined in this way is possible only to the extent that the will of men and nations can be bound to propositions and conditions hammered out around conference tables with the interests and security of participating nations in mind.

In this life, there are people who are at peace and people who appear to be at peace. There are people who commit offenses against God and trespass against their neighbor, yet are neither remorseful nor cast down in their souls. Others sin with impunity and never have a sleepless night. Some are so callous they ignore the prompting of conscience to do right. Then, there are those who cover their tracks so well and mask their feelings so effectively they appear never to experience the consequences of their behavior.

On the surface, these people appear to be at peace, but they are not, for one of the consequences of reaping what we sow is that if what we sow does not contribute to abundant living, the harvest can never be one peace, tranquility, and order.

While some individuals appear impervious to the consequences of their actions, and others capable of ignoring conscience, all who commit trespasses and offenses against God are destined to reap what they have sown. In some private, unguarded moment everyone who trespasses or commits an offense against God knows, as did David, Peter, and Judas, what it means to be cast down in one's soul.

It is interesting to contemplate the timing of Jesus' bestowal of peace. Shortly after bestowing peace upon the disciples, Jesus enters Jerusalem where His destiny will be fulfilled in Crucifixion. Three days later, He will be raised from the dead and shortly afterward, armed with the peace left them, the disciples will venture forth into the world to fulfill the commission given them.

◆   ◆   ◆

One reason peace has been such a delicate undertaking throughout history is simply that those involved in the peace process have not comprehended the difference between the peace of Jesus and the peace of the world.

Because they have not understood this difference, diplomats continue to go about the task of peacemaking by attempting to create external structures and conditions which, hopefully, will ease tensions and eliminate conflict.

Regrettably, this kind of peace is tenuous and seldom lasts. Time after time in this century efforts of those who have sought to make peace by binding the wills of men and nations to external structures and conditions hammered out around conference tables have been brought to naught by those intent upon keeping alive memories of ancient feuds and those who choose to remember sins and trespasses committed against themselves rather than forgive their trespassers.

In addition, those involved in the peace process have also failed to grasp the full significance of Jesus' statement, *"Blessed are the peacemakers."*

Peacemaking, it seems, is work. It is doing everything possible with the resources inherent in one's being to bring about an inner state of wholeness, tranquility, fulfillment, and order in oneself and those about us.

◆   ◆   ◆

So, what kind of a person makes peace? What traits and characteristics are the marks of the peacemaker?

Peacemakers are, first and foremost, people inwardly confident and secure in who they are. They possess a healthy, positive image which they present in ways that convince others they are genuine, real, and authentic.

The process of developing a self-image essential to peacemaking begins during infancy when we are most impressionable. While still in the womb, parents initiate the process of image-building by impressing the image they hold of themselves upon their children. When the image parents have of themselves is positive and constructive, children are given a leg up as far as inner confidence, security, and peace are concerned.

Of course, it would be a mistake to suggest that simply because an individual is confident and secure in who they are that he or she is destined to be a peacemaker. It would not be overstatement, however, to contend that individuals possessing healthy, positive self images are better prepared to work for peace in the lives of others than are persons of low self esteem.

It is critically important that men and women who desire to be called children of God comprehend the difference between Jesus' peace and peace as the world understands it as the direction of life for everyone is either inside/out or outside/in.

Men and women who work for the kind of peace Jesus bestowed upon the disciples live their lives from the inside/out. Because they live outward from the core of their being they are not afraid to connect spirit-to-spirit with those in whose lives wholeness, serenity, security, health, well-being, prosperity, and order are missing.

By contrast, the direction of life for men and women who work for peace as the world understands it is outside/in. And while their efforts sometimes succeeds in lessening tension and lowering conflict in their lives and the life of those around them, peace created in this way is fleeting because it is based upon the false assumption that peace can be created by external means.

While the road to peace is arduous, peacemakers connect with the spirit of others convinced they make a difference in the scheme of things. Knowing they make a difference is what enables peacemakers to withstand the pressures and influences encountered in working in the lives of others.

Until convinced that nothing outside themselves is capable of producing inner peace, men and women who live from the outside/in will, to paraphrase the words of a contemporary song, continue to seek peace in all the wrong places.

Peacemakers move gently through the world doing everything possible to become inwardly confident and secure. They work hard to be conscious and receptive of themselves, warts and all, refusing to think of themselves as failures when they are unsuccessful in some endeavor or fall short of some goal. Rather than identifying with their failure and labeling themselves failures, peacemakers simply acknowledge they have failed at something and move on, thus avoiding a disturbance of inner peace.

Peacemakers preserve tranquility and order in their own lives by refusing to take responsibility for the lives of others, at the same time demonstrating a willingness to leave conflicting parties where they are when it becomes apparent that matters have gone as far as they can go.

By virtue of their calling and the nature of sheep, shepherds are peacemakers. Shepherds of human flocks work for peace by promoting unity, cohesiveness, and oneness essential to a sense of the flock within congregations for which they are responsible.

A sense of the flock comes as members of a human flock recognize—to be all they can be—they need each other. To encourage this win/win mentality, peacemakers model what it means to be loving and caring in one's relationships, at the same time keeping the mission of the flock in the forefront rather than their personal interests.

Peacemaking shepherds recognize the ill effects striving after status, authority, and prominence has upon human flocks. They understand that when these things are sought at the expense of members of the flock the result is tension, division, and a weakening of the sense of the flock necessary for unity to prevail and groups be productive. In the mind of peacemakers, status, authority, and position are not acquired by striving. Instead, like greatness in the Kingdom of God, they are rewards that come to them that serve.

Peacemakers work for peace by endeavoring to bring about reconciliation between people and groups at odds with each other, a task that requires them to concentrate on behavior and feelings without taking sides, confronting when necessary, and stating what one believes to be truth at all times.

Those who work for peace approach situations in which conflict and strife is present wondering, "Isn't there a way of resolving this matter? "Isn't there a better or different way of looking at or thinking about this matter, a better way of feeling about something or someone, a better way of handling this situation?"

◆   ◆   ◆

F. W. Riggs raises an intriguing point when he proposes peacemaking as a kind of war, a war of faith against fear and love against hate.[5]

If peacemaking is thought of as warfare, what weapons are available?

Paul's listing of the fruits of the Spirit (Galatians 5:22) reads like a textbook of weapons available in warring for peace. What more effective tools for waging a war against fear and hate than love, joy, peace, patience, gentleness, kindness, goodness, meekness, faithfulness, temperance, and self control? (Ephesians 5:9)

Yet, if peacemaking is war, where is the battlefield? Where is the field of battle when the enemy is not a flesh and blood adversary? In a sense, the battlefield is anywhere peace is not. If peace is not in the human heart, it is there the battle must be waged. If not in the home, it is there that the war must be fought. If not encountered on the streets of our cities, it is there that the fight must be joined. If peace does not characterize relationships, that is where the encounter must take place.

And what of tactics?

What guidelines are available for fighting a war whose objective is peace with ourselves, others, and the world?

As faith, hope, and love are values that endure, might they have tactical value in such a war?

The tactical value of faith is its capacity to convince people that peace is possible, while the tactical value of hope is its ability to keep alive the vision of a future in which fear and hatred, hunger and loneliness no longer exist.

While faith and hope have great tactical value in a war in which the enemies are not flesh and blood, it was Paul's opinion that love was of the greatest tactical value to peacemakers, because *"...love endures long and is patient and kind. Love is never envious nor does it boil over with jealousy. It is neither boastful, vainglorious, or haughty. It is neither conceited nor proud, rude or self-seeking, and is not easily angered. It does not insist upon its own rights or its own way for it is not self-seeking. It is neither touchy, fretful or resentful and keeps no record of evil done to it because it does not rejoice at injustice and unrighteousness, but rejoices when right and truth prevail. It protects, trusts, hopes, perseveres, and most important, it never fails."* [Author combined paraphrase of Annotated and NIV]

In the Sermon on the Mount Jesus advocated love as a tactic for promoting peace. *"Love your enemies,"* He said, *"pray for those who persecute you."* (Matthew 5:44). From the Cross He demonstrated love as a peacemaking tactic by praying, *"Father, forgive them, for they know not what they do."* (Luke 23:34)

Love as a peacemaking tactic enables peacemakers to separate who people are (which emphasizes relationship) from what people do (about which peacemakers may have strong feelings).

The ability to make this important distinction is essential if peacemakers are to maintain focus. Being able to separate who people are from what they do is what enables peacemakers to pray for and promote dialogue with individuals, organizations, and nations who foster and thrive on the presence of fear, hate, violence, loneliness, hunger, and disorder.

Notes For Shepherds

The several factors recognized as destined to vex human sheep in the Twenty-First Century (hunger, fear, aggravation from external factors, and difficulties in relationships) point to a continuing need for shepherds skilled in the art of making peace.

Neither animal nor human sheep, it seems, can be at peace when their bellies are empty, fear rules their lives, or when frustrated or aggravated by factors in the environment or tension is present in relationships.

If shepherds, themselves, are hungry, if there is debilitating fear in their lives, if burdened by external factors, or relationships with others do not supply the support, affirmation, and encouragement needed to produce growth, it is unlikely their efforts at peacemaking will be effective.

Augustine's definition of peace as tranquility of order suggests that for shepherds to be effective peacemakers they must be at peace with themselves.

To be at peace with themselves, the theological and psychological houses of shepherds must be in order. They must be comfortable with who they are, at home with themselves physically, emotionally, intellectually, and spiritually.

Shepherds recognize inner peace and joy come anytime one is absorbed in something so completely that time is suspended and place becomes irrelevant, or so absorbed in another person that separateness is overcome and love flows unabated.

◆   ◆   ◆

In the Century that looms before us, few things are likely to obstruct inner peace as much as the pursuit of success. The difficulty with success, as with peace, lies in the fact that like peace, success has come to be viewed as something outside ourselves, therefore, something to be pursued. We speak of pursuing success rather than being a success. Because genuine peace is inner peace, to pursue it in things external is to encourage discontent, imbalance, and disorder.

Nothing said is intended to minimize success as a goal or to suggest we should not use our gifts, talents, and abilities to fullest advantage in the interest of providing for ourselves and those for whom we are responsible.

Of course, success is a worthy goal; however, success is not something to be pursued. Success is being at peace with ourselves, others, and God in the innermost part of our being, knowing nothing outside one's self is capable of bringing lasting peace and tranquility to life.

As humankind moves through the Twenty-First Century, shepherds will be presented with unparalleled opportunities for working for peace in the lives of human sheep. As needs and concerns left unaddressed and unresolved inevitably erupt in conflict and strife on some level, shepherds must be willing to connect spirit-to-spirit with human sheep, shower them with attention, and share presence with those walking through Valleys of Dark Shadows.

Shepherds must not write off human sheep when they stray from the flock. Sheep are sheep. They stray because it is their nature. They stray because some need they have has not been met, or some concern has not been addressed. Shepherds willing to go in search of members of the human flock who stray and are cast down in their souls will experience success.

To this end, shepherds must never withhold understanding, acceptance, and love from human sheep, for these qualities are like balm. They bring relief to aggravating life situations in much the same manner as salve applied to an abrasion brings relief.

Times in which the fabric of society is being rewoven and its institutions restructured are particularly stressful for human sheep and those who lead them. They require leadership of the highest caliber from those who have been called to the vocation of shepherd.

Perhaps what is needed is for shepherds to ask themselves, "In a world that threatens to stretch members of the human flock beyond their limits, how am I to shepherd human sheep in my care?"

However this question is answered, shepherds must never forget their goal is abundant life for sheep in their care. If they will address the fears of human sheep, work to eliminate hunger, lessen aggravation, and assure sheep walking through Valleys of Dark Shadows that a table of blessing awaits them, that they will yet feast in the presence of their enemies, the cups of human sheep will overflow and their desire to walk in the paths of righteousness and dwell in the house of the shepherd's God will be strengthened.

Shepherds who succeed in these areas are certain to be blessed as God will call them children of God.

10

Oh the Blessedness
of Those Are Who Are
Persecuted
for Righteousness Sake

❖

The Beatitude on the Cost
of the Kingdom of God

How interesting that Jesus should follow a Beatitude blessing those who work for peace with one that speaks of His followers being blessed because they are insulted, persecuted, slandered, and ridiculed.

Jesus did not leave his disciples in the dark about what lay in store for all who followed Him. *"In this world,"* He said, *"you will have trouble,"* (John. 16:33) and in His life and ministry He demonstrated the truth of this warning of things to come.

In Scripture, but especially, the Gospel of John, the *"world"* is understood as *"humanity, estranged from and asserting its independence of God."* [1]

In short, from the time Jesus issued His warning, His followers have known theirs would not be an altogether smooth passage through the world, that from time to time, humanity estranged from God would assert itself and the result would be trouble.

◆   ◆   ◆

Followers of Christ did not wait long for Jesus' warning to become part of their experience.

Peter and John were first to experience trouble. After healing a lame man at the gate of the Temple, Peter seizes the opportunity to proclaim the resurrection of the dead in the name of Jesus. For this he and John are brought before the elders and scribes assembled in Jerusalem and questioned by what power or in what name they had healed the man because, in the words of the elders, "they had filled Jerusalem with their teaching."

In the presence of the religious leaders of the day and the man who had been healed, Peter defends the healing as an act of kindness.

Unable to deny the miracle of healing and faced with a loss of influence, the religious leaders release Peter and John with a warning not to speak or teach in the name of Jesus.

Shortly afterward, because of the wonders and miraculous signs he had performed in Jerusalem, Stephen is brought before the Synagogue of the Freedmen and asked to give an account for himself. Unable to stand against his wisdom, members of the Synagogue persuade men to say they had heard Stephen speak words of blasphemy against Moses and God. (Acts 6:11)

As a consequence, Stephen is brought before the highest court in Judaism, the Sanhedrin, and charged with speaking words of blasphemy. When asked by the high priest if the charges are true, Stephen speaks with such force and dignity that members of the Sanhedrin drag him outside the city and stone him.

The martyrdom of Stephen ignites an outbreak of persecution against Christians in Jerusalem, scattering them in all directions. The moving spirit behind this initial persecution is Saul of Tarsus who, himself, would shortly experience the truth of Jesus' warning.

◆   ◆   ◆

Quite early in the life of the Church, believers discovered that simply being identified as a follower of Christ was sufficient to invite trouble. *"It is one of the commonplaces of history,"* writes Kenneth Scott Latourette, *"that in its first three centuries Christianity met persistent and often severe persecution..."*[2]

Trouble came initially from Jews *"antagonized by the fashion in which what superficially appeared to be a sect of Judaism was undermining institutions and convictions cherished by that religion."*[3]

With the passage of time, *"Jewish malevolence, popular slander and dislike, and political principles"* led to the persecution of Christians as enemies of the state, public enemies, and outlaws.[4]

Followers of Christ found their relationship to society and government particularly troublesome.

In this regard, it is well to ask, "How is it that men and women of the First Century came to regard followers of Christ as public enemies and outlaws? What was the nature of the threat posed by Christ's followers that society and empire alike should have viewed them as 'difficult,' electing to martyr rather than accommodate them?"

Whatever the nature of the threat, it was such that before the beginning of the Second Century, followers of Christ were martyred with such frequency that the same word *(martus)* was used for both "witness" and "martyr."[5]

◆   ◆   ◆

In any age, what is it that makes one person or group of persons difficult for others? What made followers of Christ difficult in the eyes of society and the people of the First Century? Equally important, what made society and people of the First Century difficult for Christians?

And finally, what led followers of Christ and the Roman Empire to view each other as difficult?

Generally, people (or groups of people) are difficult for each other because they:

- Perceive and approach the world differently
- Think differently
- Hold different values, or
- Have different needs and fears.

◆   ◆   ◆

Out of our experience, each one of us fashions a frame of reference or habitual way of thinking and feeling about the world, people, and what happens to us.

What this means is, anyone whose frame of reference or approach differs from our own is potentially difficult for us because they think differently than we do, their fears are different from ours, and their values are different.

For example, a short while ago, John and Janet W. were traveling to a neighboring state where John, a clergyman, was scheduled to address a conference of pastors. Nearing their destination, they were stopped by a highway patrolman. "Do you know how fast you were driving?" asked the patrolman.

"Oh, about sixty miles an hour," John replied.

At this point, Janet broke into the conversation. "John, I'm surprised at you. You were going exactly sixty-eight miles an hour!"

Unless John understands Janet's approach to the world differs from his, that her approach is one that demands exactness while his does not, he may interpret her remark as a put-down, a questioning of his integrity, or perhaps, a rebuke, in which case, conflict and hurt are likely.

While John tends to view the world adaptively (which means he is comfortable with approximates), Janet approaches the world analytically (which means her world demands exactness, preciseness, detail, and order).

To remain at peace within herself, Janet felt compelled to correct John's less than exact estimate of speed. Whereas Janet does not rest well unless the family bankbook is in balance, John is not troubled as long as they are not overdrawn at the bank.

The need of those who, like John, approach the world adaptively is to be liked, loved, accepted, and affirmed. By whom? People, of course! Their need being what it is, the worst thing that can happen to them is to experience rejection. Comfortable with generalizations and approximates, John and those like him are potentially difficult for people like Janet for whom exactness, preciseness, and detail are absolutely necessary if they are to avoid chaos in their inner world.

While John views the world adaptively and Janet views it analytically, a third group of people approach the world aggressively.

As used here, aggression does not imply intent to harm, but rather the need to control or take charge of circumstances, situations, and people. While the need of those who approach the world and people aggressively is to control, their fear is loss of control.

A fourth group of people perceives the world in a manner entirely different from those who view it adaptively, analytically, or aggressively. This group perceives the world apathetically. They are indifferent, hence, difficult for those around them because of their indifference to the world and people.

Individuals whose frame of reference is that of apathy prefer to be left alone. They live detached from people as much as possible. They shun connection, association, and attachment because such things trigger their fear of involvement.

The experience of a fifth group leads people to approach the world from the perspective of personal growth and development. The need of this group is to experience growth in wholeness, contentment, and fulfillment in all areas of life. Valuing growth so highly, the worst thing that can happen to them is for some situation or circumstance to thwart their progress as the thing they fear most is stagnation.

◆   ◆   ◆

In addition to frame of reference, perception, and needs, people are also difficult for each other because they value different things.

It has been said while we are pushed by our drives, we are pulled by our values. Values are the stars by which we navigate through life. When people value different things, they are potentially difficult to someone else as the following story illustrates.

On a chilly November evening, a black doorman hailed a taxi for a white family exiting their hotel. The brisk wind blowing that evening suddenly lifted the hat from the head of the couple's six-year-old daughter. Before anyone could stop her, the girl darted into the street in pursuit of her hat. Only the doorman was in a position to see the danger posed by an approaching bus. Moving swiftly, he ran after her and returned her safely to her parents.

What is interesting about the story is the way response to what the doorman had done revealed the values held by persons close to him.

From his wife's perspective, what the doorman did was a foolish stunt. No one with a wife and children who needed him and were dependent upon him would have done such a thing. Because she valued security, the action of the doorman was foolhardy.

The doorman's brother also disapproved of his action, mostly because the rescued child was white. "If you're going to kill yourself," said the brother, "do it for one of your own." Because he valued people who were black over those who were white, what the doorman did was foolish.

The doorman's employer, on the other hand, praised him for performing a selfless act and at year's end rewarded him with a substantial bonus. Because he valued relationships with guests, what the doorman did was selfless.

The doorman's pastor described him as a hero. Because he valued love of his fellow man, what the doorman did was heroic.[6]

◆   ◆   ◆

In the First Century, Christians were perceived as difficult because faith in Christ led them to fashion an approach to the world, society, and the Roman Empire that differed from the majority of people in the world. Rome viewed them as difficult because they valued allegiance to God above allegiance to Rome and gave ultimate authority for their lives to God rather than the Emperor.

Rome needed a rallying point around which to unify an empire of unprecedented proportions containing a host of peoples, languages, cultures, faiths, and traditions, a symbol that called to mind the benefits enjoyed under Roman rule and elicited the gratitude of the people. Respect for the Emperor was intended to be that rallying point.

While Christians respected and prayed for the Emperor, they were unwilling to swear ultimate allegiance to him, nor were they willing to acknowledge Caesar as the ultimate authority of their lives. From their perspective, followers of Christ felt they could give ultimate allegiance and authority to God at the same time remaining loyal to the Empire. It was when worship of rather than respect for the Emperor became a test of political loyalty that peace between the Empire and Christianity became impossible.

In all likelihood, had Christians been willing to affirm Caesar as Lord, charges of treason, sacrilege, and practicing magic would not have been brought against them, and Christianity would have been tolerated as other faiths were tolerated, and persecution avoided.

The difficulty, however, was Christians could not and would not elevate Caesar to the place reserved for God as that meant disregarding the First Commandment with its prohibition against having other gods before the God of Abraham, Isaac, and Jacob. Given the prevailing state of affairs, however, to go against the one who personified the Empire was the same as going against Rome itself.

Refusing to affirm Caesar as Lord, Christians were branded disloyal to the state, distrusted as traitors, viewed as potential revolutionaries, and denounced as threats to the Empire.

Refusing to engage in the daily sacrifice offered for the welfare of the Emperor and the Roman people or to participate in the compulsory act of burning incense to the Emperor and declaring loyalty to Caesar as Lord, Christians found themselves outside the law, convenient scapegoats when policies of weak emperors resulted in failure or disaster.[7]

When values held by followers of Christ ran counter to the personal interests of powerful segments of society, Christians became threats to special interest groups who brought pressure upon administrators to act against them.

◆   ◆   ◆

The doctrine of the Eucharist proved a major source of trouble for Christ's followers.

Matthew records that on the night He was betrayed, that Jesus took bread, gave thanks and broke it, and gave it to his disciples, saying, *"Take and eat; this is my body."* Then, continues Matthew, Jesus took the cup, gave thanks and offered it to the disciples, saying, *"Drink from it, all of you. This is my blood of the covenant, which is poured out for many for the forgiveness of sins."* (Matthew 26:26-27)

Eating bread (understood as the body of Christ) and drinking wine (understood as the blood of Christ) brought charges of cannibalism against Christians. Celebrating the Eucharist only in the presence of believers brought the charge that Christians regularly sacrificed infants and consumed their flesh and blood.[8]

Because Christian worship involved eating and drinking and took place at night, engaging in orgies was another charge leveled against early Christians. *"At their nocturnal gatherings, solemn feasts and barbarous meals,"* wrote one non-Christian writer, *"the bond of union is not a sacred rite but crime.... These conspirators must be destroyed and cursed."*[9]

◆   ◆   ◆

From the discussion of the ways people become difficult for each other, it seems apparent that when individuals or groups of people approach the world the same way, value the same things, and have similar needs, they pose no threat to each other. However, when individuals or groups perceive the world differently, hold different values, and have different needs, they are potentially difficult for each other.

Because Christians approached the world differently than people of the First Century, held different values, and because their needs differed from the needs of society and the Empire, they were considered difficult, and trouble, persecution, and martyrdom followed.

◆   ◆   ◆

Scripture presents trouble as inevitable, and persecution, a distinct possibility for those who follow Christ. This being the case, what stance are followers of Christ to take when simply being a disciple is a source of trouble?

On what grounds are Christians to rejoice when adherence to the Gospel brings persecution, trouble, and suffering?

What is there about doing what is right and being persecuted for it that makes one worthy of the blessing of God?

Finally, in what sense is the Kingdom of Heaven reward for those who endure persecution for righteousness' sake?

The only plausible reason for rejoicing when adherence to the cause of Christ brings trouble and persecution is found in the phrase, "for the sake of righteousness."

Apart from righteousness there is little, if any, cause for rejoicing when reviled and persecuted, harassed, snubbed, rejected, put-down, discriminated against, and all manner of evil is said against one falsely.

Had Jesus not told His followers to rejoice and be exceeding glad, indeed, leap for joy when trouble comes, it would be quite easy to dismiss those who do as odd, strange, or at a minimum, different.

The word translated "exceeding glad" comes from the verb *agalliasthai* derived from two Greek words which mean "to leap exceedingly."[10]

To be exceeding glad is to experience the emotional high climbers exhibit upon reaching the summit of Mount Everest, the elation athletes feel upon winning the gold medal in Olympic competition, the deep, inner satisfaction that an individual feels who has just learned he or she has been awarded the Pulitzer Prize in their field, the joy of knowing that the person you love most, loves you as well.

However, to an age more inclined toward getting even than forgiving those who trespass against them, the idea of rejoicing and being exceeding glad in times of trouble seems terribly naive.

And while it doesn't make good sense to rejoice as if trouble were something to be welcomed, it does make sense to rejoice "in" experiences of trouble. We rejoice in times of trouble and difficulty because it is at such times that we learn things about God, ourselves, and others previously unknown or inexperienced that become catalysts of growth.

In times of trouble and difficulty, we rejoice

• By praying for those who persecute us and

• By forgiving those who sin and trespass against us.

Exercising the freedom that is ours of choosing our response to trouble and difficulty enables us to exercise self-mastery and self-control, remain objective, hence, more inclined to forgive than attempt to get even with those who trespass and commit offenses against us.

But, what of persecution and trouble that comes because Christians invite it upon themselves?

The fact remains that some Christians are prone to court trouble and invite persecution. Some perceive themselves duty bound to give a witness in all situations, however inappropriate it might be. Others bring reproach upon themselves and the Gospel by parading their faith before men in ways that call attention to themselves. Still others invite trouble by forcing the Gospel into situations in which the cause of Christ is more likely to be mocked and derided than advanced.

Notes to Shepherds

"In this world you will have trouble." These words are certain to prove true for followers of Christ in the Twentieth-First Century as they did in the First Century.

It seems unlikely that followers of Christ should escape trouble during periods of rapid change and transition as their frame of reference is different from that of a majority of society's people, their perception of the world and people is different, and their values are inner-directed rather than external.

So, how are shepherds to minister effectively in a world in which they are difficult for some people because of the nature of the Gospel, a world in which they and the sheep they lead are not exempt from trouble, persecution, and/or martyrdom?

Equally important, how are shepherds to minister effectively in situations in which from time to time, the very things that render followers of Christ difficult in the eyes of those about them also lead shepherds and human sheep to view each other as difficult?

◆   ◆   ◆

If shepherds are to be effective in the care and management of human sheep, and as much as possible, avoid seeing those they serve as difficult and being viewed in the same way, it is essential that they learn to understand and meet the needs of people.

Earlier, it was said that out of our experience we fashion a frame of reference that prompts us to perceive the world and people the way we do.

To understand and meet the needs of people, it is essential that shepherds acquaint themselves with the several ways people approach their world, for in the way people perceive their world they reveal their (a) primary need, (b) primary fear, (c) the way they recognize and demonstrate love, and (d) within reason, where they can be found in the work place.

1. The Growth View

Some people view the world as an arena of personal growth and development. Their need is to grow and develop in all areas of life. They feel important and needed as long as they are moving in the direction of wholeness, completeness, and self-mastery while not growing in these ways triggers their primary fear, which is stagnation.

Balanced and in control of themselves, those who view the world in this way are often found in the diplomatic corps or among industry's top executives because they have the ability to meet the needs and act in the best interest of people, organizations, or country, and do what must be done, in spite of how they feel.

2. The Adaptive View

The need of people who view the world adaptively is to be liked, loved, accepted, and affirmed. They feel important when shown love, affirmation, and acceptance. When these things are not forthcoming, fear of rejection is triggered. Consequently, people who view the world through adaptive lenses are attracted to occupations (such as teaching, clergy, nursing, and counseling) in which people contact is extensive, but occupations in which rejection and limited success are part of each day.

3. The Analytical View

Exactness, preciseness, and detail are the needs of people who view the world analytically. Drawn to occupations in which the ability to be exact and precise is a strength and attention to detail is required (engineering, architecture, banking, and computers among others), these people are secure when everything is in order, things are precisely where they ought to be, and every detail is tended to. To them, disorder is chaos.

4. The Aggressive View

A fourth group views their world aggressively. Their primary need is to control situations and people. They feel important when they are in charge. We find members of this group protecting and serving society and its people as policemen. They drive the eighteen-wheelers that bring our goods to the marketplace. They serve us in Congress, and interestingly enough, they swell the ranks of the criminal element.

5. The Apathetic View

The need of the Apathetic is to be left alone. Their primary fear is involvement. Individuals who view the world apathetically have as little to do with people as possible. Their names swell the ranks of those on welfare, those who are institutionalized, and those who are incarcerated, contexts in which contact with the world is minimal.

◆   ◆   ◆

If shepherds will learn to identify the way(s) human sheep view the world, and commit themselves to meeting the needs and acting in the best interests of sheep in their care (without triggering their fear), not only will they be effective in their shepherding, the possibility of becoming difficult in the eyes of the people they serve will be minimized.

Let's permit John, the pastor whom we met earlier, to demonstrate how the ability to identify the way people view the world can be useful to shepherds of human sheep.

As John is adaptive in his approach to people and the world, he prefers preaching life-situation sermons with heavy emphasis upon liking, loving, accepting, and affirming others and experiencing these things in relationship to God.

It is a simple fact of life that when our needs are met, we feel loved, and when they are not met, our fears are triggered. Therefore, should John fail to recognize his needs are not those of at least fifty percent of the congregation, in time he will viewed as difficult by a significant segment of the congregation because their needs are not being met.

Should the needs of these people remain unmet for an extended period, the chances are good they will cease responding to John in ways that say to him, "You are liked, loved, accepted, and affirmed."

Minus the affirming, accepting, loving responses of the congregation, John is likely to feel unappreciated and unimportant, perhaps rejected, and some of the joy will go out of his work.

John must also recognize that some members of his congregation, his wife among them, are analytical in their approach to the world. To meet their needs John will need to preach sermons that focus on doctrines of the faith and sermons that provide detailed instructions for living the Christian life.

Assuming John's congregation is representative of society in general, there will undoubtedly be a number of people who approach the world aggressively, whose needs are best met in a kind of direct, forceful sermon known generally as "hell-fire-and brimstone."

People whose need is to control find sermons of this kind to their liking because it is in sermons of the hell-fire-and-brimstone variety that the Gospel most directly confronts issues of sin and injustice of the world. It was by means of this kind of message that the prophets sought to recall Israel to worship of the true God.

Speaking through the prophet Jeremiah, Jehovah addressed the issue of Israel's following after other gods in passages that left no doubt that it was His intention to take charge of a situation He found unacceptable. *"Because your fathers have forsaken me…and have walked after other gods, and have served them, and have worshiped them, and have forsaken me…I will cast you off this land."* (Jeremiah 16:11)

Few opportunities for ministering to people who approach the world apathetically are likely to come John's way as these people seldom attend services of worship. To meet their need to be left alone John must avoid being overly aggressive in inviting them to services of worship or attempting to involve them in ministries of the Church as that would trigger their fear, which is involvement on any level.

◆　　　◆　　　◆

John's task as shepherd is to become so confident and secure in himself that he willingly commits himself to meeting the needs and acting in the best interests of every member of the congregation, though their needs and concerns are not his own. To do this, John will need to learn what love is, and commit himself to loving others in ways they are prepared to receive love.

John will demonstrate love by preaching sermons in which he encourages people to grow rather than stagnate. He will deliver sermons that say to people, "The message of the Gospel is God loves, accepts, and affirms you."

He will address the issues and circumstances of living in an aggressive, ambitious society in sermons that provide detailed instructions for bringing order out of a social, cultural chaos.

He will speak to issues of sin and injustice directly and aggressively that people will know God is in control and that, like Christ, they too can overcome the world.

He will address the apathy and fear of some members by allowing the power of his presence to draw them into a more active, and productive, participation in the world.

And when trouble and difficulty come to members of the congregation, John will rejoice with them in their experiences knowing God works in all things for that which is good, namely, that those who follow him might be more like His Son.

Epilogue

Somewhere in his passage modern man has departed from the purpose of God. Responding to social forces reweaving the fabric of society, restructuring its institutions, and stretching people to the limits of their adaptability, society and its people have let go, lost, or left behind a number of important beliefs, traditions, practices, and principles called "roots" that not only served as guidelines for their lives, but which brought continuity and consistency to life.

Minus these stabilizing guidelines, modern man does not know what he wants to say with his life; therefore, he seeks meaning, purpose, direction, and a sense of personal worth and value in things external to himself rather than within.

To live the abundant life, man must return to the Purpose of God.

To do that, man must reclaim his status as a spiritual being and commit himself to a way of life that places value on the inner life of the spirit.

He must come to a fresh appreciation of presence as an attribute of his humanness, as the cornerstone of relationships, as a comforting, reassuring, validating power when connected with the spirit of others.

He must make a critical assessment of technology, once again begin to play with purposeless abandon, and reclaim time as a measure of life rather than a product.

He must seek to become poor in spirit, pure in heart, meek, and merciful; willing to mourn with his neighbor when difficulties come, work for peace in his own life and that of others, and hunger and thirst after righteousness.

If modern man will do these things he will be blessed with all the good things of the Kingdom.

About the Author

Dr. Charles E Smith is an author, lecturer, conference leader, and a licensed Marriage, Family, and Child Counselor.

He has spent his adult life working with individuals in a variety of settings ranging from the classroom and consultation room to the conference hall, presenting subjects ranging from self-esteem to after-care.

Active in his community and church, and several times a grandfather, Dr. Smith lives with his wife, Norma, in Poplar Bluff, Missouri.

Other Titles by Dr. Charles E. Smith
Come Teach Your Lambs
Growing Gold
Growing Gold Through Grief
Helping Children Cope With the Death of a Parent
Growing in Self-Esteem
New Beginnings for Single-Parent Families
Commitment: The Cement of Love

Contact Information
www.GrowingGold.com
DrSmith@growinggold.com

References

Chapter One

[1]Elmer Mould, *Essentials of Bible History* (New York: The Ronald Press Company, 1951), p. 9.

[2]Alvin Toffler, *Future Shock* (New York: Bantam Books, 1970), p. 12.

[3]Ibid.

[4]Ibid.

[5]William Bridges, *Transitions* (Menlo Park, California: Addison-Wesley Publishing Company, 1980), p. 5.

[6]Paul Roberts, "Goofing Off," *Psychology Today*, (July/August, 1995), p. 40.

[7]Rhoda Thomas Tripp (compiler), *International Thesaurus of Quotations* (New York: Harper & Row, 1970), pp. 971-972.

[8]Roberts, op. cit., p. 41.

[9]Ibid., p. 39.

[10]Ibid., p. 34.

[11]Richard Nisbett, *The Idea of Progress in History* (New York: Basic Books, 1980), p. 353.

[12]Anne Wilson Schaef and Diane Fassell, *The Addictive Organization* (San Francisco: Harper and Row, 1988), p. 4.

[13]Charles E. Smith, *New Beginnings For Single-Parent Families* (New York: Carlton Press, Inc., 1993), pp. 80-82.

[14]John Powell, S.J., *Why Am I Afraid To Tell You Who I Am?* (Niles, Illinois: Argus Communications, 1969), p. 20.

[15]Arthur Green, Henry Work, and Diane Schetky and others, "Violence Said To Be Part Of Child's Life," *Marriage and Divorce Today*, (March 3, 1986), p. 1.

[16]Ibid.

[17]Ibid.

[18]Ibid.

[19]Melinda Beck and others, "In A State Of Terror," *Newsweek*, (September 27, 1993), p. 40.

[20]George Buttrick (editor), *The Interpreter's Bible, XIV* (Nashville: Abingdon Press, 1952), p. 126.

Chapter Two

[1]David Spangler, *The Call* (New York: Riverhead Books, 1966), p. xiii.

[2]Charles E. Smith, *New Beginnings For Single-Parent Families* (New York: Carlton Press, Inc., 1993), p. 62.

[3]Ibid.

[4]Christina Maslach, *The Cost of Caring* (Englewood Cliffs, NJ, 1982), p. 3.

[5]Eugene Kennedy, "Why A Good Friend is Hard To Find," *U.S. News and World Report*, September 26, 1983, p. 71.

[6]Wayne Oates, "A Christian's Interpretation of Sex," *The Young People's Teacher*, (October 1963), pp. 10-12. *The Young People's Teacher* is a publication of the Southern Baptist Convention published by Broadman Press, Nashville, Tennessee.

[7]Abraham Maslow, *Motivation and Personality*, (New York: Harper & Row, 1970).

[8]"Sex Is What?" *Common Sense Communicator* (Clayton Stahlka, editor), n.d., p. 3.

[9]Monica McGoldrick, Carol M. Anderson, and Froma Walsh (editors), *Women In Families* (New York: W. W. Norton and Company, Inc., 1989), pp. 357-358.

[10]John Powell, *He Touched Me* (Niles, Illinois: Argus Publications, 1974), p. 74.

[11]Ibid., pp. 70-74.

[12]Ibid., pp. 54-55.

Chapter Three

[1]Spiros Zodhiates, *The Complete Word Study Dictionary*. (Iowa Falls, Iowa: World Bible Publishers, Inc., 1992), pp. 937-938.

[2]William Barclay, *The Daily Study Bible, Vol. I* (Philadelphia: The Westminster Press), p. 84.

[3]Zodhiates, op. cit., pp. 519-520.

[4]William Barclay, Plain *People Look At The Beatitudes* (Nashville: Abingdon Press, 1993), pp. 17.

[5]Ibid., pp. 16-17; Zodhiates, op. cit., p. 1253.

[6]James Hastings (editor), *Hastings Dictionary Of The Bible* (2nd.ed.; Hendrickson Publishers, 1994), pp. 741-742.

[7]Zodhiates, op. cit., p. 1181.

[8]Martin Luther, *Greek-English Lexicon of the New Testament* (Grand Rapids: Zondervan, 1982), p. 520.

Chapter Four

[1]Bertha Simos, *A Time To Grieve* (New York: Family Service Association of America, 1979 p. 1.

[2]Myron Chartier, "Christian Marriage: What is It?", *Marriage and Divorce Today* (no date), pp. 14-16

[3]William Barclay, *The Daily Study Bible, Vol. I* (Philadelphia: The Westminster Press), p. 89.

[4]Elmer Mould, *Essentials of Bible History* (New York: The Ronald Press Company, 1951), p. 403.

[5]Barclay, op. cit., p. 90.

[6]Mould, op. cit., p. 277.

[7]Ibid.

[8]James Hastings (editor), *Hastings Dictionary Of The Bible* (Hendrickson Publishers, 1994), p. 361.

[9]Dietrich Bonhoeffer, *Letters and Papers From Prison*, ed. Eberhard, Bethge, (New York: Simon and Shuster, 1997) p. 191

Chapter Five

[1]William Barclay, *Plain People Look At The Beatitudes* (Nashville: Abingdon Press, 1993), pp. 34-35.

[2]James Hastings (editor), *Hastings Dictionary Of The Bible* (New York:Hendrickson Publishers, 1994), pp. 601-602.

[3]Barclay, *loc.cit*; Spiros Zodhiates, *The Complete Word Study Dictionary* (Iowa Falls, Iowa: World Bible Publishers, Inc., 1992), p. 1208.

[4]Gary Collins, *Christian Counseling: A Comprehensive Guide* (Waco: Word Books Publisher, 1980), pp. 100-101.

[5]Jay E. Adams, *The Christian Counselor's Manual* (Nutley, Jersey: Presbyterian and Reformed Publishing Company, 1973), pp. 349-350.

[6]Herbert Lockyear, Sr., *Nelson's Illustrated Bible Dictionary* (Thomas Nelson Publishers, 1986), p. 302; James Hastings, op. cit., p. 233.

[7]Ibid

[8]Ibid.

[9]Ibid.

[10]Beverly Flanigan, "Unforgivable War Crimes Of The Heart," *Psychology Today* (September-October, 1992), p. 39.

[11]The Creed of Optimist International was written by Christian Slater.

Chapter Six

[1]Paul J. Achtemeier, *Harper's Bible Dictionary* (San Francisco: Harper, 1985), p. 808; James Hastings, (editor), *Dictionary Of The Bible* (New York: Hendrickson Press, 1994, p. 742.

[2]Hastings, op. cit., p. 728; Achtemeier, op. cit., p. 795.

[3]Spiros Zodhiates, *The Complete Word Study Dictionary* (Iowa Falls, Iowa: World Bible Publishers, Inc., 1992), p. 1457.

[4]Ibid., p. 773.

[5]John Powell, *He Touched Me* (Niles, Illinois: Argus Publications, 1974), p. 63.

[6]William Barclay, *The Daily Study Bible, Vol. I* (Philadelphia: The Westminster Press), p. 97.

[7]William Barclay, *Plain People Look At The Beatitudes* (Nashville: Abingdon Press, 1993), pp. 52.

[8]Fleming James, *Personalities Of The Old Testament* (New York: Charles Scribner's Sons, 1939), p. 517.

[9]Dwight Lowell Dumond, *Antislavery Origins of the Civil War* (Ann Arbor: University of Michigan Press, 1963), p. 5.

[10]Ibid. p. 42

[11]Dwight Lowell Dumond, *Antislavery, The Crusade For Freedom In America*. Ann Armor: University of Michigan Press, 1961. Chapter Twenty-Three contains an excellent review of the life and work of Birney.

[12]Ibid. Chapter Twenty-One is a survey of Theodore Weld's participation in the antislavery movement, particularly his role in the enlistment and training of antislavery agents.

[13]Ibid. Chapter Twenty-Two is an account of Angelina Grimke's involvement in the antislavery movement.

[14]Barclay, *Plain People*, p. 55.

Chapter Seven

[1]Karen Armstrong, Jerusalem, *One City, Three Faiths* (New York: Alfred A. Knopf, 1996), p. xvi.

[2]*Webster's New Universal Unabridged Dictionary* (New York: Simon & Shuster, 1983, p. 1126.

[3]Ibid.

[4]Paul J. Achtemeier, *Harper's Bible Dictionary* (San Francisco: Harper, 1985), p. 626.

[5]William Barclay, *The Daily Study Bible, Vol. I* (Philadelphia: The Westminster Press), p. 98.

[6]Spiros Zodhiates, *The Complete Word Study Dictionary* (Iowa Falls, Iowa: World Bible Publishers, Inc., 1992), p. 563.

[7]Elmer W. K. Mould, *Essentials of Bible History* (New York: The Ronald Press, 1951), p. 252.

[8]Bill Blackburn, *Understanding Your Feelings* (Nashville: Broadman Press, 1983), p. 33.

[9]Rollo May, *Power and Innocence* (New York: Norton, 1971), pp. 105-113. May's discussion of five kinds of power (among them nutrient and integrative power) is recommended as helpful tools for demonstrating compassion and mercy) and their uses.

[10]Hastings, op. cit., p. 605.

[11]Ibid.

Chapter Eight

[1]William Barclay, *Plain People Look At The Beatitudes* (Nashville: Abingdon Press, 1993), pp. 72-73.

[2]Ibid.

[3]Madeleine S. and J. Lane Miller, *Harper's Encyclopedia of Bible Life* (Edison, New Jersey: Castle Books, 1978), p. 15.

[4]Herbert Lockyer, Sr., *Nelson's Illustrated Bible Dictionary* (Nashville: Thomas Nelson Publishers, 1986), p. 632.

[5]Paul J. Achtemeier, *Harper's Bible Dictionary* (San Francisco: Harper, 1985), p. 994.

[6]Frederick Carl Eiselen, Edwin Lewis, and David G. Downey, *The Abingdon Bible Commentary* (Nashville: Abingdon Press, 1929), p. 962.

[7]Barclay, op. cit., p. 79.

[8]Miller, op. cit. p. 258-261

[9]Ibid., p. 260.

[10]Ibid., p. 261.

[11]Robert Schuller, *The Be(Happy) Attitudes* (Waco: Word Books Publishers, 1985), p. 121-133.

[12]Spiros Zodhiates, *The Complete Word Study Dictionary* (Iowa Falls, Iowa: World Bible Publishers, Inc., 1992), p. p. 729.

[13]Ibid. p. 924.

Chapter Nine

[1]Frederick Carl Eiselen, Edwin Lewis, and David G. Downey, *The Abingdon Bible Commentary* (Nashville: Abingdon Press, 1929), p. 1067.

[2]Joseph F. Pfeiffer, Howard Vos, and John Rea (editors), *Wycliffe Bible Dictionary* (Hendrickson Publishers, 1999), p. 1300-1301; James Hastings (editor), *Hastings Dictionary Of The Bible* (Hendrickson Publishers, 1994), p. 696.

[3]Spiros Zodhiates, *The Complete Word Study Dictionary* (Iowa Falls, Iowa: World Bible Publishers, Inc., 1992), p. 519.

[4]D. Stuart Briscoe, *Spirit Life* (Old Tappan, New Jersey: Fleming H. Revell Company, 1978), p. 49.

[5]F. W. Riggs (mimeographed). This expression of the meaning of peace was sent to the writer by a friend who found it in the bulletin of his church.

Chapter Ten

[1]William Barclay, *Plain People Look At The Beatitudes* (Nashville: Abingdon Press, 1993), p. 98.

[2]Kenneth Scott Latourette, *A History of Christianity* (New York: Harper & Brothers, 1953), p. 81.

[3]Ibid.

[4]Barclay, op. cit., p. 109.

[5]Ibid., p. 97.

[6]Every effort has been made to find the biographical source of this story. Even the hotel chain for which the doorman worked was contacted. The story was included because it is a concrete example of what makes people difficult for each other.

[7]Paul Johnson, *A History of Christianity* (New York: Simon and Shuster, 1976), pp. 70-71.

[8]Latourette, op. cit., p. 82.

[9]Johnson, op. cit., p. 70.

[10]William Barclay, *The Daily Study Bible*, Vol. I, (Philadelphia: The Westminster Press), p. 112.

Bibliography

Achtemeier, Paul J. (General Editor). *Harper's Bible Dictionary*. San Francisco: Harper, 1985.

Adams, Jay. *The Christian Counselor's Manual*. Nutley, New Jersey: Presbyterian and Reformed Publishing Company, 1973.

Armstrong, Karen. *Jerusalem, One City, Three Faiths*. New York: Alfred A. Knopf, 1996.

Barclay, William (Translator*). The Daily Study Bible*. 17 vols. Philadelphia: Westminster Press, 1956.

Barclay, William. *Plain People Look At The Beatitudes*. Nashville: Abingdon Press, 1963.

Beck, Melinda and others, "In A State Of Terror," *Newsweek*, September 27, 1993, pp. 40-41.

Blackburn, Bill. *Understanding Your Feelings*. Nashville: Broadman Press, 1983.

Bonhoeffer, Dietrich. *Letters and Papers From Prison*, ed. Eberhard Bethge. New York: Simon and Shuster, 1997.

Bridges, William. *Transitions, Making Sense of Life's Changes*. Reading, Massachusetts: Addison-Wesley Publishing Company, 1980.

Briscoe, Stuart. *Spirit Life*. Old Tappan, New Jersey: Fleming H. Revell Company, 1978.

Buttrick, George (editor), *The Interpreter's Bible.* 12 Vols. Nashville: Abingdon Press, 1952.

Chartier, Myron, *Marriage And Family Living,* "Christian Marriage: What Is It?", pp. 14-16.

Collins, Gary. *Christian Counseling.* Waco: Word Books Publisher, 1980.

Dumond, Dwight Lowell. *Antislavery, The Crusade for Freedom In America.* Ann Arbor: The University of Michigan Press, 1961.

Dumond, Dwight Lowell. *Antislavery Origins Of The Civil War In America.* Ann Arbor: University of Michigan Press, 1963.

Eiselen, Frederick Carl, Edwin Lewis, and David G. Downey. Nashville: Abingdon Press, 1929.

Flanigan, Beverly. "Unforgivable War Crimes Of The Heart," *Psychology Today,* (September/ October, 1992), pp. 36, 38-39, 78-79, 90-92.

Green, Arthur, Henry Work, and Diane Schetky. "Violence Said To Be Part Of Child's Life," *Marriage and Divorce Today,* March, 1986, p. 1.

Hastings, James (editor). *Dictionary Of The Bible.* 2nd ed. New York: Hendrickson Press, 1994.

James, Fleming. *Personalities of the Old Testament.* New York: Charles Scribner's Sons, 1939.

Johnson, Paul. *A History of Christianity.* New York: Simon and Shuster, 1976.

Kennedy, Eugene, "Why A Good Friend Is Hard To Find," *U.S. News and World Report,* (September 26, 983), p. 71.

Latourette, Kenneth Scott. *A History Of Christianity.* New York: Harper & Brothers, 1951.

Lindsey, Karen. *Friends as Family: New Kinds of Families and What They Could Mean For You.* Boston: Beacon Press, 1981.

Lockyer, Herbert, Sr. (General Editor), *Nelson's IIllustrated Bible Dictionary.* Nashville: Nelson Publishing Company, 1996.

Maslach, Christina. *Burnout, The High Cost of Caring.* Englewood Cliffs, N.J.: Prentice-Hall, 1982.

Maslow, Abraham, *Motivation and Personality,* (New York: Harper & Row, 1970)

May, Rollo. *Power and Innocence.* New York: Norton, 1971.

McGoldrick, Monica, Carol M. Anderson, and Froma Walsh (editors). *Women In Families* (New York: W. W. Norton and Company, Inc., 1989.

Miller, Madeleine S. and J. Lane. *Harper's Encyclopedia of Bible Life.* Edison, New Jersey: Castle Books, 1978.

Mould, Elmer W.K. *Essentials of Bible History.* New York: The Ronald Press, 1951.

Nisbett, Richard. *History of the Idea of Progress.* New York: Basic Books, 1980.

Oates, Wayne. "A Christian's Interpretation of Sex," *The Young People's Teacher,* (October 1963), pp. 10-12. The Young People's Teacher is a publication of the Southern Baptist Convention published by Broadman Press, Nashville, Tennessee.

Optimists International

Powell, John. *He Touched Me*. Niles, Illinois: Argus Communications, 1974.

Powell, John. *Why Am I Afraid To Tell You Who I Am?* Niles, Illinois: Argus Communications, 1969.

Riggs, F. W. (mimeographed). This expression of the meaning of peace was sent to the writer by a friend who found it in the bulletin of his church.

Roberts, Paul. "Goofing Off," *Psychology Today*, (July/August, 1995), pp. 34-41.

Schaef, Anne Wilson, and Diane Fassell, *The Addictive Organization*, (San Francisco: Harper and Row, 1988), p. 4.

Schuller, Robert. *The Be(Happy) Attitudes*. Waco: Word Books Publisher, 1985.

Simos, Bertha. *A Time To Grieve*. New York: Family Service Association of America, 1979.

Smith, Charles E. *Growing In Self-Esteem*. New York: Carlton Press, Inc., 1993.

Smith, Charles E. *New Beginnings For Single-Parent Families*. Poplar Bluff, Missouri: Stinson Press, 1993.

Spangler, David. *The Call*. New York: Books, 1996.

Stahlka, Clayton (editor), "Sex Is What?" *Common Sense Communicator*, n.d., p. 3.

Thayer, Joseph Henry, *Greek-English Lexicon of the New Testament*. Grand Rapids, Michigan: Zondervan Publishing House, 1982.

Toffler, Alvin. *Future Shock*. New York: Bantam Books, 1970.

Tripp, Rhoda. *International Thesaurus of Quotations.* New York: Harper & Row, 1970.

Waldman, Steven, "Deadbeat Dads," *Newsweek* (May 4, 1992), pp. 46-51.

Webster's New Universal Unabridged Dictionary. New York: Simon & Shuster, 1983.

Zodhiates, Spiros. *The Complete Word Study Dictionary.* Iowa Falls, Iowa: World Bible Publishers, Inc., 1992.

0-595-23638-3